Chicago

A Pictorial Celebration

Dennis H. Cremin, Ph.D.

Photography by Elan Penn

Sterling Publishing Co., Inc.
New York

Design by Michel Opatowski
Edited by J. E. Sigler
Layout by Gala Pre Press Ltd.

Library of Congress Cataloging-in-Publication Data
Cremin, Dennis H.
Chicago : a pictorial celebration / Dennis H. Cremin ; photography by Elan Penn.
p. cm.
ISBN 1-4027-2387-3
1. Chicago (Ill.)-History. 2. Chicago (Ill.)-Description and travel. 3. Chicago
(Ill.)-Pictorial works. 4. Historic buildings-Illinois-Chicago. 5. Historic
Sites-Illinois-Chicago. I. Penn, Elan. II. Title.

F548.3.C74 2005
977.3'11-dc22

2005048945

2 4 6 8 10 9 7 5 3 1

Published by Sterling Publishing Co., Inc.
387 Park Avenue South, New York, NY 10016
© 2006 by © Penn Publishing Ltd.
Distributed in Canada by Sterling Publishing
c/o Canadian Manda Group, 165 Dufferin Street
Toronto, Ontario, Canada M6K 3H6
Distributed in Great Britain by Chrysalis Books Group PLC
The Chrysalis Building, Bramley Road, London W10 6SP, England
Distributed in Australia by Capricorn Link (Australia) Pty. Ltd.
P.O. Box 704, Windsor, NSW 2756, Australia

Printed in China

Sterling ISBN 1-4027-2387-3

For information about custom editions, special sales, premium and
corporate purchases, please contact Sterling Special Sales
Department at 800-805-5489 or specialsales@sterlingpub.com.

Opposite: Cloud Gate, by Anish Kapoor, 2004. Located in Millenium Park.

 Contents

Chicago Learns: Cultural Contributions to the World . .110

Chicago Plays: Enjoying the Past, Present, and Future . . .126

Index 160

Chicago in 1831. View of Fort Dearborn and (from left to right) homes of John Dean, J. Baptiste Beaubien, Dr. Wolcott, and John Kinzie. Library of Congress Prints and Photographs Division, Washington, D. C..

Chicago's grid of streets is home to a wonderful array of stories. The major story line started around 10,000 years ago, when the glaciers of the last ice age began to retreat from the North American continent. As they scoured the land, they flattened much of what would one day make up Illinois, scraped out the holes that would become the Great Lakes, then filled them up by melting. In time, the wind deposited rich soil here, and eventually Native Americans moved onto this land. They found abundant animals to hunt and grew squash, beans, and maize in their "three sisters" gardens.

The very name of the city is taken from a Native American word, either the Algonquin word for a pungent weed that grew in the swampy land, or the Potawatomi word "Checaugou," which some assert referred to a wild onion that grew in the area.

This name, as well as the name Illinois, are two of the very few traces left by the area's first inhabitants. The city arose so quickly that even the first Europeans in the area did not manage to leave many lasting marks on the landscape. As in many American cities, Chicago's first European visitors

were explorers and traders who met with Native Americans, traded goods with them, and left. Jean Baptist Point du Sable, a Caribbean trader of African descent who came here in 1779, is believed to be the area's first permanent settler.

Du Sable's little trading post grew into a small settlement on the American Western frontier of the early 1830s. Then, in less than a century, that little village grew into a metropolis of over one million people. Already by the 1890s, Chicago had risen to the status of America's second largest city in population (second to New York City). Chicago is now considered *the* American City of the Midwest, and it has lived up to that prestigious status. It has fundamentally transformed the region's landscape, revolutionized the lives of Americans several times over, and today it is a world leader in manufacturing, banking, and culture, and a national and international hub for transportation and trade. How it got there—and where it's going next—are the fascinating stories told by the city's streets themselves.

Chicago Works: Forging the Future from the Prairie

In the 1950s, Mayor Daley—who arguably has had more influence on the development of the modern city than any other single individual—called Chicago "the City that Works." As much as he was describing his vision for the modern city, Daley was also describing Chicago's hardworking past. From downtown today, it is difficult to picture the city's earliest history, but the land on which Chicago sits was once nothing more than a low-lying, swampy area. Located at the intersection of the Great Lakes and the Mississippi River watershed, the site's exposed shoreline and muddy shores were inhospitable, to say the least.

Out of that mud, however, rose the great metropolis one sees today—or rather, it *was raised* by the sweat and brawn of many a Chicago worker. By 1848, just 15 years after the inhabitants incorporated the town, Illinoisans like John Deere and Cyrus McCormick had already radically transformed the state's landscape, and the Chicago Board of Trade had revolutionized agricultural economics. These events are the stuff of myth within Illinois. It is almost as if Vulcan was hammering out reapers, and Ceres, the goddess of wheat, had provided the abundant harvest.

As Chicagoans seemed to gain complete mastery over their environment, it seemed like a bolt from Zeus when much of the central city burned in what has come to be called the Great Fire of 1871. Now remembered by the Chicago Fire Memorial at the Chicago Fire Academy, the fire burned for several days over three and a half square miles, destroyed 18,000 structures, killed around 300 individuals, and left many, many more homeless. Because of this disaster, there are only scattered remnants of early Chicago around the city today. One of the most important is the Henry B. Clarke House from 1836, one of the oldest homes in Chicago and probably the best remaining example of the city's early settlement. The most symbolic remnant of those days is the historic Water Tower, which itself helped to fight the fire. The water works—of which the tower is the most imposing part—demanded considerable labor. Workers had to dig under the lake to fresh water sources, quarry the limestone of which the enormous edifice is constructed, and then transport it to the site.

To the astonishment of the world, Chicago rebuilt quickly after the fire, asserting its resourcefulness and resolve as it began creating a new city upon the still-smoldering ashes of the old. During this time and up through the 1890s, the city experienced a period of unprecedented economic growth and expansion, becoming the national capital of such iconic industries as animal slaughtering, meat packing, and shipping. The city became known as "the hog butcher to the world," a role exemplified by the Union Stock Yards entrance.

At the same time, Chicago was gaining a reputation as the creator of the first skyscrapers. This history is found in many early structures, including the Monadnock Building, one of the first buildings to demonstrate Chicago's ability to be an innovator in the field of architecture. This ability would become one of the city's hallmarks in the years to come, as some of the world's most innovative architects chose Chicago as their playground. During the building boom of the 1920s, for example, Frank Lloyd Wright revolutionized domestic architecture in nearby Oak Park. His Robie House in Hyde Park, with its horizontal

"The Great Fire at Chicago, October 9th 1871." Image circa 1871. Library of Congress Prints and Photographs Division, Washington, D. C..

lines and art glass windows, has become the symbol of the Prairie Style. After World War II, both Chicago's cityscape and the world's architectural consciousness would be heavily impressed upon by the design and teaching of Ludwig Mies van der Rohe. The buildings at Chicago Federal Center reflect Mies' design sensibility, and they now serve as the icon of Chicago's second great school of architecture.

Chicago's most recent innovations reflect a different sensibility entirely. 333 Wacker Drive, for instance, which reflects the curve of the Chicago River in its green-glass façade, is the harbinger of a "river revival"—just one expression of a newfound, popular appreciation for all the city's natural resources, which it once shamelessly polluted. In a very different way, the expansion of McCormick Place, the city's convention center, embodies that same lesson learned: after the first building was criticized as an eyesore along the lakefront, the new additions known as McCormick Place North and South were built away from the water. This is how Chicago's buildings tell the story of Chicagoans themselves: the city's architectural works of art are not just an expression of some architect's whims, but reflect the sentiments of the citizens themselves at a particular point in the city's history. They are a product of the people's loves and loathings, of the lessons they have learned, and most of all, of their own labor.

Chicago Moves: By Water, Earth, and Air

The "river revival" reflected in 333 Wacker Drive has induced more and more people to appreciate—and to enjoy—Chicago's waterways. Few people appreciate the importance of the Chicago River and Lake Michigan to the city's history, however. Many people see Lake Michigan every day, and may cross the Chicago River as many as three or four times a day, but most have little sense that it was the water itself that provided the impetus for the development of the city.

In fact, the site on which Chicago is located actually had little to recommend it. Except for one thing, that is: its location right smack in the heartland of the country, and right at the mouth of the Chicago River on the shores of Lake Michigan. This location made it possible to connect the Great Lakes to the Mississippi River through the Chicago River and other, smaller waterways. In a time in which waterways were

Bird's-eye view of Chicago from Lake Michigan, circa 1892. Library of Congress Prints and Photographs Division, Washington, D. C..

the primary means of transportation, this simple fact provided the foundling city with great strategic and economic importance.

For early visitors to the Midwest, the site became a prime location to "portage" canoes through "mud lake"—as the area just a few miles south of today's city center was then called—which allowed travelers to cross a glacial moraine that separates the waters of the Great Lakes from the Mississippi basin. The mouth of the Chicago River rapidly became a major center in the fur trading business, and the first traders' settlements grew up on the shores now overlooked by the Michigan Avenue Bridge. This early history is commemorated in one of Henry Hering's bas reliefs on the bridge, *Pioneer Chicago*, which depicts the first European settlers in the area.

Upon recognizing the strategic importance of the site, the U. S. federal government secured the area with a fort, and later built a pier into Lake Michigan, making Chicago one of the best harbors on the lake. In 1847, Chicago completed the 96-mile-long Illinois and Michigan canal as well, which linked New York to New Orleans through Chicago's shores. After the Civil War, the laying of the first railroad tracks through the American Midwest even further solidified Chicago's status as the crucial link tying together the "civilized" nation in the east with its wild and untamed frontier out west. The city in the heartland gained a reputation as a central meeting place for the nation because of its many rail lines, and it became host to a great number of important national events. Chicago is still the national hub for Amtrak, the United States' passenger rail line, but these days most people come into Union Station. Completed in 1925, Chicago's Union Station was the last of the nation's great rail stations to be built.

Since Chicago already tied the nation together by water and rail, and since many early roads passed near Chicago, it came as no surprise to Americans that Route 66 would begin there. A sign marking the start of Route 66 stands on Adams Street just off of Michigan Avenue. The "mother road" is still a much-beloved symbol of freedom and mobility in the United States. Completed in the 1920s, the route linked Chicago to Los Angeles, cutting through America's southwest. It marked the ascent of the automobile in American society, enabling people to drive great distances at heretofore never-conceived-of speed.

These days, the automobile is the American way to travel, and most Americans are not very familiar with water or rail travel anymore. Many Chicagoans, on the other hand, still feel right at home on a boat or train. For very long distances, though, they tend to travel just like other Americans: by plane. After World War II, railroad usage began declining in the United States in general, and so the city began expanding its airports. As most anyone who has ever flown cross-country already knows, Chicago's status as national hub—once by waterway, next by rail, then by road—still holds today by air.

Chicago Gathers: Out of Many Neighborhoods, One City

All the workers it took to build up Chicago and all her houses, skyscrapers, bridges, and roads—they might be the one thing that did *not* seem to just rise out of the prairie. They built up their own communities, too, and at their centers usually stood one structure: the church. Chicago is well known as a city of neighborhoods, and these neighborhoods were often demarcated by Catholic, Protestant, or Jewish affiliation. Churches and synagogues for Chicago's immigrants served not just as a place of prayer and worship, but as a gathering place for Catholics, Protestants, and Jews from "the Old Country," as a support system and a place to network and receive guidance.

Interestingly, church architecture often recreated the familiar environment of the land of emigration in Chicago's new immigrant communities. For example, Old Saint Patrick's Church, the city's oldest neighborhood church, is a window onto the communities of early immigrants from Ireland and Germany. Similarly, Holy Trinity Russian Orthodox Cathedral's traditional Eastern Orthodox design

The famous "White City": exposition grounds of the World's Columbian Exposition, 1893. Library of Congress Prints and Photographs Division, Washington, D. C..

seems to Westerners like an import from another planet, making the cathedral one of the city's best examples of the diversity of cultures that came—and still come—to build Chicago.

Pilgrim Baptist Church, originally built as Kehilath Anshe Ma'ariv (KAM) Synagogue, demonstrates how Chicago neighborhoods were continually settled and resettled by newcomers. Built between 1890 and 1891, the KAM synagogue became home to Chicago's oldest Jewish congregation, which dates back to 1847. As the Jewish residents of the neighborhood became more established with time, they moved away, and the area was slowly occupied by new African-American immigrants from the south. In 1926, they converted the old synagogue into Pilgrim Baptist Church.

First Presbyterian Church in Lake View exemplifies changes not in neighborhood demographics, but in city geography. At the time of its construction, it was outside the city limits, and so it could be built with a wood frame, which had been banned within the city limits after the Great Fire. Not long after the church went up, though, the neighborhood was woven into Chicago's urban fabric.

Chicago Marvels: Great Events that Shaped the City

Just as the early settlement of Chicago had to be physically raised out of the mud, Chicago's business elite began to elevate the city culturally in the 1890s. In 1893, their activities brought the World's Columbian Exposition to Jackson Park, a celebration of Columbus' arrival in America 400 years earlier. This event, more than any other, was the turning point in Chicago's history, and it still exerts its influence over the city and its inhabitants to this very day.

While it is an overstatement to say that the exposition introduced culture to Chicago, it did transform the cultural landscape of the city. The "White City," as the collection of the exposition's white neoclassical buildings came to be known, provided an alternative vision to life in the dark, coal-burning, industrial city of the period. The exposition established the neoclassical style as the city's favorite, setting an architectural trend for its cultural institutions. In the wake of the fair, the central city would be greatly improved by the addition of an expansive park—Grant Park—and the eventual extension of the shoreline. There are still quite a few monuments within the city that link to this great period in history, including the Statue of the Republic, the Museum of Science and Industry, the Art Institute of Chicago, and the Field Museum of Natural History.

Most importantly, the vision embodied by the fair was the seed of a commitment to improve the lives of everyday citizens through dynamic civic planning—a commitment the city has kept to its citizens ever since. When the Great Depression descended on the nation in 1929,

Chicago marched onward, doing perhaps the exact opposite of what one expected: it threw itself a grand birthday party. Even as the economic trouble deepened, Chicago hosted another fair in 1933 named "Century of Progress," since its incorporation as a town in 1833. Though the fair was only intended to last a year, it was so successful that it was extended through 1934. By the end of its run, 39 million people had made their way to the fair. The Christopher Columbus Statue in Grant Park is a remnant of that celebration, hearkening back in theme to the World's Columbian Exposition of 1833.

Most recently, the city reclaimed twenty-four and a half acres of railroad lands and parking lots on the northern end of Grant Park in order to carry out there a multimillion-dollar experiment in public-private partnership. Thankfully, the result has been incredibly successful: Since 2004, visitors from near and far have come to Chicago just to see the new Millenium Park. The park is a complex feat of engineering, as commuter rail lines still run underneath it and most of the park is built on top of underground parking. This was intentional, however, and part of the city's ingenious plan for financing the improvements: revenue from the parking lots helps pay for the park. The "enhancements"—the best part of Millenium Park—were largely funded through private donations.

The centerpiece of the park is Frank Gehry's much-beloved Pritzker Pavilion, now the new home to the Grant Park Music Festival. Jaume Plensa's Crown Fountain redefines the function of a fountain in an urban setting, and Anish Kapoor's sculpture *Cloud Gate* (locally known as "the bean") is a wonder of contemporary art. It has become the most popular sculpture in the city—perhaps even the nation. Both Kapoor's sculpture and Plensa's fountain reveal the underlying motive behind Millennium Park and Chicago's other great events: not just to improve the city for its citizens, but to encourage the citizens to interact with their city.

Chicago Learns: Cultural Contributions to the World

The sense that the city was undergoing a cultural awakening at the time of the World's Columbian Exposition was further reinforced by the founding

State Street, one of the busiest streets in the world, circa 1903. Library of Congress Prints and Photographs Division, Washington, D. C..

Poster advertising Buckingham Fountain, shown before the Chicagos skyline. Federal Art Project, 1939. The Library of Congress Prints and Photographs Division, WPA Poster Collection.

of The University of Chicago in the same decade. It seems interesting to many visitors that, although the university boasts the most Nobel laureates from its faculty, graduates, and researchers of any university in the United States, the campus seems shrouded in medieval-looking buildings. The design was intentional, however, and is actually quite practical. Henry Ives Cobbs designed the campus' original 17 buildings in the Gothic Revival style in order to guarantee stylistic harmony between buildings throughout the campus. The plan made it possible for future buildings to be integrated into the campus without standing out for their modernity. Eckhart Hall, for instance, which was added to the campus in 1930, cannot be distinguished in age from the Former Walker Museum, one of Cobbs' original 17.

The city's cultural renaissance reached beyond art into the sciences, and Chicago has carried on a legacy of nuclear innovation and leadership ever since the first atomic fusion took place on the University of Chicago campus in 1942. Today, Henry Moore's sculpture *Nuclear Energy* marks the spot from which the scientist Enrico Fermi thrust America and the world into a new age of science and technology. This breakthrough and those that followed in its wake gained Chicago considerable renown as a great scientific force. At the same time, the Illinois Institute of Technology (IIT) was emerging as a world leader in engineering and technology, largely thanks to the German architect Ludwig Mies van der Rohe, the groundbreaking architect who fled Nazi Germany for the United States. Mies' legacy at IIT is visible not just in the modernist design of its campus buildings, but in the school's excellent architecture and design programs.

The city's Museums in the Park, which include the Adler Planetarium and Astronomy Museum, the John G. Shedd Aquarium, and new additions like the Mexican Fine Arts Center Museum, cemented Chicago's reputation as a city of great culture and learning. The museums are known not just for their exhibits and events, but also for their profound contribution to the world in the areas of research and interpretation.

Chicago Plays: Enjoying the Past, Present, and Future

Besides its great location, architecture, and culture, Chicago has a reputation for knowing how to have a good time. Its outdoor sculpture, well-tended parks, authentic food, original music, and serious sports prove that the city that works hard can play hard just as well—maybe even better. Ever since the creation of the city's earliest parks, including Lincoln Park, Chicago has been expanding and improving its public parklands and entertainment facilities. A shortage of space is usually the greatest challenge for civic planners in beautifying the urban area, but Chicago has proven very adept at finding the perfect spot to realize every good idea. Lincoln Park itself was converted from a municipal cemetery, and Navy Pier—a historic structure that dates back to World War I, but which was once in a state of dilapidation—is now one of the city's greatest success stories.

Chicago is renowned for its sports parks, too. It is home to both one of the oldest baseball parks in the nation, Wrigley Field, and one of the newest, Soldier Field. "The Friendly Confines" of Wrigley Field, as the park is known, are as alluring to fans for their historic features as for the games played there. The park has been one of the most successful sites in the city at blending past, present, and future. Soldier Field's construction of a new stadium within its historic colonnades, on the other hand, has met with mixed reviews. Most are impressed by the new stadium as a sports facility, but the changes obliterated much of the historic fabric of the early building—so much that some say the new building looks like a spaceship landed in the colonnades.

Over 100 years ago, the German Berghoff Restaurant started a Chicago culinary tradition of authentic eateries, of which the most famous are still the Chicago-style pizzerias. The Billy Goat Tavern is also an heir to that tradition, as well as a hallowed Chicago institution, made famous locally by the articles of *Chicago Tribune* journalist Mike Royko, and nationally by a favorite *Saturday Night Live* skit. Leon's Bar-B-Q and White Palace Grill are two more of the most appreciated (and frequented), but the great variety of restaurants in Chinatown and other ethnic and immigrant neighborhoods around town all contribute to Chicago's reputation as a city of distinctive eateries.

As much as its authentic food—and perhaps even more so—Chicago's distinction as the birthplace of electric blues has earned it an honored position on the scales of world music history. Willie Dixon's Blues Heaven, formerly the site of the Chess Records recording studio, played a pivotal role in earning the city this status. In tribute both to the city's history as a great blues town and as an innovator in all things musical, Blue Chicago, Double Door, Green Mill, Velvet Lounge, and others of Chicago's newest

Poster advertising Adler Planetarium, beneath stars, planets, and constellations. Federal Art Project, 1939. Library of Congress Prints and Photographs Division, WPA Poster Collection.

musical venues all strike a balance between classic and contemporary sounds.

All these great forms of classic Chicago entertainment attract millions of visitors to the city each year. Many sites are not just for the city's citizens, though, but part of a larger American heritage. Aware of its importance to the development of the nation—and now of the world—Chicago is a city greatly enamored of its past, and both tourists and locals love to visit its most historic and famous sites to witness firsthand the story of the swampy trading post that American ingenuity and frontier spirit transformed into this world-class metropolis. Granted, Chicago is not a paradise, but there is a sense that it is heading in the right direction. Its residents exude confidence, its leaders uphold its legacy of constant improvement, and together they are able to express that civic spirit in bold and innovative ways. That is the history of Chicago, and the Chicago legacy.

Chicago Works: Forging the Future from the Prairie

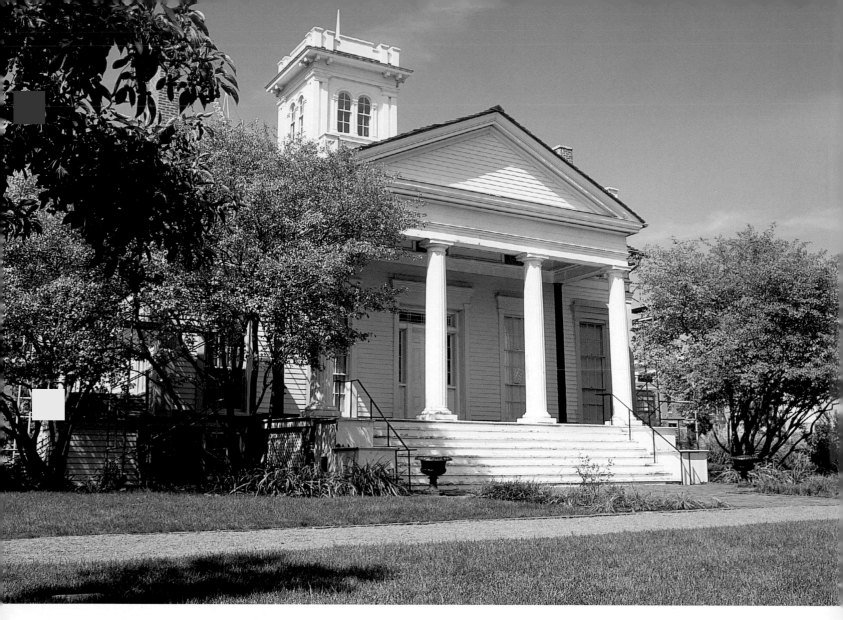

The Henry B. Clarke House and Museum

The Clarke House is just enough off the beaten path to be left off many visitors' lists of sites to see, but it is an excellent example of Chicago's early settlement. It is one of the oldest homes in Chicago, built in 1836, and thus predating even the incorporation of the city in 1837. When this home was still new, in 1840, only 4,470 people called Chicago their home.

In its day, the Clarke house must have made quite an impression with its pristine white exterior and Greek Revival architecture. Even today, the home makes a statement, illustrating just how prosperous many of Chicago's earliest merchants became. The structure has been moved a couple of times: It originally stood near 16th Street and Michigan Avenue, but in 1871

the owners moved it to 45th Street and Wabash Avenue on the city's south side. Then in 1977, the City of Chicago acquired the house and moved it to its present location at 1855 South Indiana, just one block southeast of its original location.

Today, the city runs the restored Clarke House as a museum, with an interior reflecting the period from 1836 to 1860. The house also serves as an anchor of the city's Prairie Avenue Historic District, which became one of the most fashionable neighborhoods in the city in the late nineteenth century, when it featured the homes of the likes of retail giant Marshall Field and George Pullman, who gained fame for his Pullman Palace railroad car.

Previous page: Sunset over the Chicago River, as seen from the Franklin Street Bridge.

Chicago Fire Monument

Tucked away southwest of the Loop (as Chicago's downtown is called), Egon Weiner's Chicago Fire Monument at 558 West DeKoven provides great insight into the city's early history. This is the location where local tradition has it that Mrs. O'Leary's cow kicked over a lamp on a warm and extremely windy October night in 1871. The result was one of the great conflagrations in United States history: a fire that burned for 36 hours and devastated the city of around 300,000 inhabitants. While some citizens woke and immediately fled from the onrushing flames, others stayed and fought the fire for hours. The statistics from the fire are still staggering today: three and a half square miles were burned, 18,000 structures were destroyed, and around 300 individuals were killed. Many citizens were left homeless and took up temporary residence in the city's parks and outlying communities.

In spite of the shocking magnitude of the devastation, Chicago remained composed. The city again displayed its great civic spirit and determination and started to rebuild even as embers still smoldered in the city. Today, the site of the fire's outbreak is home to the Chicago Fire Academy, where trainees learn the latest techniques to prevent and fight fires. Visitors to the area can see many fire engines parked behind the building. The Fire Monument in front was sculpted in 1961 by the Viennese immigrant Egon Weiner, and has become his most famous work. The highly stylized flames reflect both the amazing nature and the potential danger of fire. On the sculpture's base are inscribed the words: "Here Began the Chicago Fire of 1871." For locals passing by the fire academy, the monument is a potent reminder of the event that marked the end of Chicago's early history.

The Water Tower

Chicago's Water Tower is a great symbol of the city's rise from the ashes of the Great Fire of 1871, which destroyed much of the city center, but left this structure standing. William W. Boyington, the prominent early architect best known for the Joliet, Illinois prison (1858), designed the limestone water tower and nearby pumping station in the Castellated Gothic style.

As much as it is a monument to the city's great optimism and perseverance in the wake of the fire, the water tower is a testament to the effort and determination of Chicago's laborers. They not only quarried the limestone for construction and erected the towering structure, but also had to tunnel under Lake Michigan to bring fresh water to the city. Although taken for granted now, clean water was not easily available in the mid-nineteenth century. Early Chicagoans used the Chicago River as their primary port, and it became an open sewer for the city's burgeoning industries. As a result, periodic bouts of waterborne disease swept through the city. The water tower eliminated this threat by drawing water from intakes far out in Lake Michigan's clean water. To this day Chicagoans continue to depend on Lake Michigan as the main source of water for the city and much of the metropolitan area.

Some locals believe that the tower is haunted by one of those determined laborers, a tale visitors to the city are likely to hear. They tell of a heroic worker who—rather than fleeing for his life—manned the Water Tower's pumps during the Great Fire of 1871. The story has it that, just before the flames reached him, he hanged himself in the structure rather than be burned to death. Some even go so far as to say that they have seen the silhouette of a man hanging inside of the tower. As far as city historians can tell, these stories appear to be a combination of a little truth and a great deal of fiction.

Union Stock Yards Entrance

Few visitors to Chicago make their way down to 850 W. Exchange Avenue to the great gate that was once a part of the city's Union Stock Yards, made famous in Upton Sinclair's novel *The Jungle*. Opened on Christmas day in 1865, the butchering grounds spread over 475 acres and became the embodiment of the industrial urban spread—and pollution—of nineteenth-century Chicago. The arched entrance recalls the days when Chicago was "hog butcher for the world" and refrigerated rail cars sent dressed meats all across the country.

The city's central location had long made it an obvious center of national trade and transportation. With the innovation of the refrigerated rail car, the area became known as a processing center for many forms of livestock. The "disassembly plant" at the Union Stock Yards gained a reputation as a model of efficiency, with every worker trained to perform a single task and utilizing, as they say, "everything but the squeal." During the World's Columbian Exposition, famous for its "White City" of white marble-like exhibit buildings, many visitors to the city made their way to the stock yards to see the efficiency of the work.

The entrance that stands today provided access to the great animal pens, where the animals were kept until slaughter. The central gateway had iron bars that descended each night, and the southern archway still has its original hinged iron gate. A bas-relief steer over the central arch is the head of Sherman, the star bull that won the American Fat Stock Show in 1878. The bull was named after John B. Sherman, founder of the Stock Yard and Transit Company.

Although a long-time staple industry for the city, the importance of Chicago's stock yards was undercut when the trucking industry replaced the railroad as the primary means of transporting livestock and a decentralized system of packinghouses began meeting demand further west. After years of decline, the Union Stock Yards finally closed in 1971. It is estimated that the market had handled more than one billion animals.

Chicago Board of Trade Building

Located at 141 W. Jackson Boulevard, the present Chicago Board of Trade (CBOT) building dates from 1930, when it was designed by the architectural firm of Holabird and Root. The history of the institution stretches back to the city's earliest days, however, when businessmen founded the Chicago Board of Trade in 1848. Today, the building is evocative of the importance of bulk commodities in the history of the city.

On the La Salle Street side of the building, Illinois artist Alvin Meyer created figures holding wheat and corn, reflecting the amazing transformation of Illinois and the Midwestern landscape that Chicago entrepreneurs induced. Illinois provided the tools to replace the many kinds of prairie grasses with wheat and corn, transforming the prairies from a diverse ecosystem to one that promoted mono-agriculture. The thick prairie soil was cut and gouged by plows manufactured in Illinois by John Deere and Company, and machines made by Cyrus McCormick did the harvesting.

As Chicago transformed the relationship of man to nature, the CBOT fundamentally transformed the relationship between agriculture and commerce by turning nature into "commodities." After the introduction of the grain elevator, an innovation that made transporting and storing grain drastically easier, farmers no longer brought their produce into city centers, not knowing if they would be able to sell their produce there. Rather, they would transport their grain to elevators, where it would be stored. Upon delivery, the quality of a farmer's grain was graded and the farmer received a receipt. His grain was then stored in bins with grain of like quality grown by other farmers. No longer would grain be bought and sold by the sack—it would be stored by the ton, moved by steam-powered machines, and flow like a river of gold.

With this new development, grain and corn became commodities, and all that abundant Midwestern harvest could now be traded—in Chicago. The CBOT was key to the success of this transition: it created the grading system for grain, contracted with the grain elevators, and, ultimately, helped set the prices for grain from around the world for international buyers who bid on its future price. Symbolizing the importance of such agricultural breakthroughs to the CBOT's success is sculptor John Storrs' aluminum statue of Ceres, the Roman goddess of agriculture, who seems to watch over all from her perch on top of the building.

To this day, Chicago remains the world's largest commodities exchange, setting prices for goods around the world. Even in this age of high-speed, long-distance communication, traders still gather in the pits of the Board of Trade from early in the morning to trade on the future prices of everything from grain, orange juice, and "pork bellies" to silver and gold. Visitors with reservations can view the often frenetic buying and selling, and there are interpretive displays that highlight the history of the CBOT and make its activities understandable to non-traders.

The Monadnock Building

Even though the state of Illinois is expansive, Chicago's downtown suffered from rather limited space. The central business area was hemmed in by Lake Michigan and the Chicago River, and the proliferation of railroad tracks and stations only exacerbated the situation. As a result, Chicago began building up early on.

The Monadnock Building, located at 54 W. Van Buren Street, is one of Chicago's earliest remaining skyscrapers. The building's unusual name, taken from one of New Hampshire's White Mountains, was considered quite appropriate for the towering edifice. The word "monadnock" is also a geological term for a mountain surrounded by a glacial plain, making it truly the perfect name for a mountain of a building in Chicago, the city so famously scoured by glaciers thousands of years ago.

The Monadnock Building is divided into four connecting sections that, side by side, provide a wonderful opportunity to see the development of technology. The two northern sections were designed by Burnham and Root utilizing the traditional masonry technique of thick, load-bearing walls. Since their completion in 1891, the two sections' 16 stories of brick have remained the tallest masonry structure in the city. The two southern sections of the building were built by Holabird and Roche in 1893. They utilized the new technology of the steel frame for this half of the building, which does not require thick walls and so looks very sleek beside the masonry structure. The steel is sheathed with terra cotta, adding to the exterior attractiveness of the entire building. At the time of its construction, Chicagoans were not used to—and, it was assumed, were unwilling to—scale what seemed to them endless flights of stairs, and so the Monadnock's architects made sure to install a safety elevator that serviced all four sections of the building.

Photo Copyright: Graham, Anderson, Probst & White, Corp.

Jane Addams Hull House Museum

The Jane Addams Hull House Museum is located at 800 S. Halsted Street. The house's name came from its main building, which Charles J. Hull constructed in 1856. When Jane Addams and Ellen Gates Starr first opened Hull House in 1889, they introduced a totally new vision for supporting the city's poor and underserved. Building on the model provided by Toynbee Hall, a settlement house in London, the two women created the most famous institution of the Progressive Movement in America.

In a city full of immigrants that all too often lived in dire poverty, the settlement house offered social, cultural, and educational opportunities. It assisted people in creating new lives for themselves, an overwhelming and sometimes nearly impossible task in the newly industrial city. For example, people could take courses on food preparation or learn technical skills, and the site provided a community lending library. Eventually, the budding charity that began as a single house grew into a complex comprising thirteen buildings.

Perhaps the best-known American woman during her lifetime, Addams wrote extensively about her experiences as a social worker before the time of social workers, and her book *Twenty Years at Hull House* attracted a great deal of attention. In recognition for her work, Addams won the 1931 Nobel Peace Prize.

Today, Hull House is operated as a museum on the campus of the University of Illinois, Chicago (UIC). The museum offers programs and preserves the history of those who worked in and utilized the settlement house.

The Frederick C.
Robie House

Tours →
Bookshop

The Frederick C. Robie House

Frank Lloyd Wright's Robie House at 5757 S. Woodlawn Avenue is perhaps the best example of Chicago's Prairie Style of architecture. Although many of Wright's Prairie Style homes were built in the village of Oak Park, Chicago's Robie House has become the symbol of this style, as well as one of the most famous homes in the world. At the beginning of his career, Wright served as an apprentice in Louis Sullivan's office. Both men were interested in creating an American form of architecture, but it was Wright who would become the quintessential American architect.

Wright designed Robie House for Frederick C. Robie, a bicycle manufacturer and automobile enthusiast. Completed in 1909, it is among the last of his Prairie Style homes. Shortly before the house's completion, Wright closed his Oak Park studio and went to Europe, leaving his associates to complete the project. Nevertheless, the house embodies much of Wright's radical thinking, which transformed domestic architecture in America. His vision was primarily horizontal, and that line is achieved by the use of long, narrow Roman bricks. Many of the interior rooms are cantilevered, creating the sensation that they are floating above the ground. Wright's attention to detail included the design of the house's furniture and art-glass windows. Throughout the design, Wright drew on the colors found in the Illinois prairie, which related the building to its natural landscape.

The Robie House eventually came into the possession of the nearby University of Chicago. Today, the Frank Lloyd Wright Preservation Trust, in partnership with the National Trust for Historic Preservation, is undertaking a long-range restoration plan, which it began in 1997. The Frank Lloyd Wright Preservation Trust also operates the Frank Lloyd Wright Home and Studio in Oak Park.

Victory

At South King Drive and 35th Street stands Leonard Crunelle's statue *Victory*, honoring the dead of the United States Army 370th Infantry, 93rd Division. This African-American World War I unit was based out of the 8th Regiment Armory, which was the first African-American armory in the United States. (It still stands just a few blocks away from the monument.) The unit traced its proud history back to the 1871 formation of the Hannibal Guard volunteer militia, which later became a division of the Illinois National Guard. During World War I, the unit was incorporated into the 370th U.S. Infantry.

The white and bronze monument is the most famous landmark of Chicago's African-American community. The Chicago *Defender* newspaper campaigned for the monument for a number of years, until it was finally erected in 1927 by the State of Illinois and the South Park Commission. The mere fact that the monument was a memorial to African-American soldiers was already extremely significant at the time, but *Victory* took on even greater meaning in the context of postwar lynchings. Particularly in the south, a great number of African-Americans were lynched after the war, including a number of men who were hung wearing their army uniforms.

The sculptor, Leonard Crunelle (1872–1944), was born in a town near Lens, France, that was destroyed in World War I. He created three life-size figures for the monument: one of an African-American soldier, one of an African-American woman symbolizing motherhood, and a figure of Columbia holding a tablet that records the location of the regiment's principal battles. The granite column and architectural setting were the result of collaboration with architect John Nyden. This main portion of the monument was dedicated amid great fanfare on Armistice Day, 1928. Crunelle wasn't finished, though: eight years later he added a uniformed World War I African-American soldier to the top of the monument. It is this figure that earned the monument its nickname "Doughboy," a term that was used to identify soldiers during World War I.

To this day, the monument is the focus of a Memorial Day ceremony, where surviving members of the "Fighting 8th" gather to honor the memory of their fallen comrades. The monument also serves to mark the Grand Boulevard neighborhood, locally known as Bronzeville. A number of neighborhoods established themselves in the years before World War I, among them the Bronzeville neighborhood. In the 1890s, most of the city's blacks lived here, and by 1920 they made up 32 percent of the area's 76,703 residents. The neighborhood has become known for its black-owned businesses, churches, and civic organizations. A few of the notable figures from this area include Andrew "Rube" Foster, founder of the Negro National Baseball League; Ida B. Wells, a civil rights activist, journalist, and organizer of the NAACP; and Louis Armstrong, trumpet player and jazz leader, who performed in many of the area's clubs.

Cook County Building / Chicago City Hall

The Cook County Building and Chicago City Hall are two separate buildings that share a monumental neoclassical façade. The building is centrally located on an entire block bounded by LaSalle, Randolph, Clark, and Washington, with the entrance to the county building at 118 N. Clark Street, and city hall at 121 N. La Salle Street. It took the architectural firm of Holabird and Roche three years, from 1906 to 1911, to erect the imposing structure.

In style, the façade is reminiscent of earlier neoclassical structures in Chicago, such as the Art Institute of Chicago (1894) and the Chicago Cultural Center (1893-97), but its scale is more comparable to the mega-façade at the Field Museum of Natural History. It features seventy-five-foot-high columns with Corinthian capitals that are the size of an entire floor, and neoclassical bas-relief sculptures on its façade that hearken back to the republican government of Rome. At the entrance on Clark Street are two sculptures inspired by figures from Michelangelo's Medici Chapel. Other bas-relief sculptures around the building depict symbols of Cook County.

Chicago, of course, is the largest city in the state and the county seat. Cook County was named for Daniel P. Cook, the first attorney general of the state of Illinois and a representative in Congress from 1819 to 1827. Chicago is infamous as the site of often rough-and-tumble politics, and the building has become rather well known as the nucleus of it all. It has been the backdrop for quite a few dust-ups and conflicts between the mayor and aldermen, as well as countless squabbles between politicians. Lately, however, passers-by haven't seen anything more exciting than Mayor Daley or some other politicians walking into and out of the building.

An interesting innovation that is not readily visible is the building's roof garden, a refreshing bit of green in the densely built area. Along with a few gardens atop other buildings in the city, this one is a pilot project that will hopefully determine whether or not the gardens cool the buildings in the summer and insulate heat in the winter. The project has the support of Mayor Daley, who has gained a reputation for promoting bike paths and green areas in the city.

Allegorical bas relief by Herman Atkins MacNeil at the Cook County Building's main entrance on Clark Street.

Nathan Hale Statue

The Nathan Hale Statue, sculpted by Bella Pratt (1867-1917), stands in front of the Tribune Tower near the Michigan Avenue Bridge. Hale volunteered in 1776, just after the outbreak of the Revolutionary War, to cross enemy lines to gather information on British Troops. He was captured and, just before his execution, is purported to have uttered the famous words, "I only regret that I have but one life to lose for my country." With this, he came to embody the high ideal of patriotism.

Hale's placement in front of Tribune Tower is not incidental, but a reflection of the patriotism of another man, the Tribune's long-time editor and publisher Robert R. McCormick. During World War I, McCormick served as the commander of the 1st Battalion, 5th Field Artillery, of the First Division. McCormick named his private estate in Wheaton, Illinois, Cantigny, after the first American battle of World War I, and today it houses the First Division Museum.

Those who stop to investigate the Hale Statue are often distracted by something about the Tribune Tower itself. In the 1920s, reporters and other people started to bring stones from all over the world to be included in the building's façade. Today the building features rocks from all 50 states, as well as unusual stones from other countries, including one from the Great Wall of China. One of the most intriguing rocks is from the surface of the moon, but it is displayed in a high security window inside the Tribune Tower. Today, the tower houses the *Chicago Tribune*, WGN-Radio, and the Tribune Company's corporate offices.

The Merchandise Mart

The Merchandise Mart, located at 111 N. State Street, reflects a great tradition in Chicago that bigger is better. Located on the north side of the Chicago River, the store's 4.2 million square feet of space take up two whole city blocks, making it the world's largest building at the time of its construction. The architectural team of Graham, Anderson, Probst and White, which designed the Wrigley Building in the 1920s, completed this elegant behemoth in the 1930s, a lasting impression of the boldness of Chicago in the years during the Great Depression.

With Chicago's reputation for meat packing, railroads, and immigrant neighbor-hoods, it is easy to overlook the city's central role in the development of retail business and the department store. Marshall Field and Company built The Merchandise Mart to be their flagship wholesale store. Today, the building is run by Merchandise Mart Properties, Inc. (MMPI), a company special-izing in the operation of buildings with wholesale showrooms. The store's 4 million square feet are now divided into display areas for wholesale goods, spaces for furniture and art furniture shows, and apparel displays. The Merchandise Mart offers building tours, which meet in the elegant entry area of the building.

The William Wrigley, Jr., Building

A central icon of Chicago, the William Wrigley, Jr., Building is conspicuously located on the Chicago River near the Michigan Avenue Bridge at 400 and 410 N. Michigan Avenue. Locally known simply as the Wrigley Building, it was erected from 1919 to 1924 by the architectural firm of Graham, Anderson, Probst and White. With the development of the Magnificent Mile—Chicago's newest retail area, featuring flagship stores and wonderful spaces to stroll in—the Wrigley Building became the symbol of the new downtown center.

The building strikes a delicate balance between monumental and human scales. Its white terra-cotta façade is a shining example of the union of the 1893 World's Columbian Exposition's bold vision with 1920s technology. The building is hard to miss, especially when lit up at night, and has become one of the most beloved structures in the city. To visitors, it is striking, unmistakable proof that they've arrived in a refined urban center. When considered together, the Wrigley Building and the Tribune Tower across the street provide a significant gateway to the city's north side, recalling the opulence of Chicago in the 1920s.

William Wrigley, Jr., came to Chicago in 1891. He sold soap and baking powder, but the item that made him a fortune and allowed him to expand his small concern into a major business was chewing gum. Wrigley became part-owner of the Chicago Cubs baseball team in 1919, and the following year became the team's major owner. In 1926, Cubs Park was renamed Wrigley Field in his honor.

Chicago Federal Center

Chicago Federal Center, located on Dearborn Street between Adams Street and Jackson Boulevard, is one of the city's great urban spaces. At the heart of the center is Federal Plaza, a wonderful open space that is a refreshing change from the surrounding urban grid. Alexander Calder created the plaza's monumental steel figure, entitled *Flamingo*. The enormity and modernity of the sculpture are right at home in the midst of skyscrapers, but its bright, unusual color and dramatic curves contrast sharply with the straight black lines of the buildings, adding interest and excitement to the whole center.

Surrounding the plaza are three buildings designed by Ludwig Mies van der Rohe, who gained fame for his work at the Illinois Institute of Technology. Van der Rohe came to be the major force in Chicago architecture in the decades after World War II, and so it was no surprise when the United States General Services Administration commissioned him to build its new administrative and judiciary buildings in Chicago. Upon completion in 1974, many Chicagoans rejected the center as a cold, inhuman landscape. Others, however, rejoiced in the Federal Center's modernist lines and extraordinary height. In a city that had constructed most of its important edifices in the glorious-looking neoclassical style, the Federal Center set a markedly different trend.

Since the federal government is owner of the Chicago Federal Center, the area is often the site of political demonstrations. Sure to go down in history is the 2003 protest against the U.S. war in Iraq, during which over ten thousand protest marchers surrounded the Federal Center. They then marched down Lake Shore Drive, where they were confronted by police. Ultimately, the police arrested 550 individuals. The plaza is perhaps less exciting—but still fun—when it becomes the site of one of the city's farmers' markets in the summer months.

The Prudential Building

The Prudential Building, located at 130 E. Randolph Street, was a much-celebrated addition to the Chicago skyline when it was completed in 1955. Designed by the architectural firm of Naess and Murchy, it was not only the first skyscraper completed in Chicago after the Great Depression and World War II, but the new tallest building in the city. As is often the case with a city's tallest building, the Prudential featured an observation deck at its opening, from which some of the most wonderful views of the city in general, and of Grant Park in particular, could be seen. High up on the building is Prudential's trademark, *Rock of Gibraltar*, sculpted by Alfonso Iannelli. Since the 1890s, the company—which is said to be "founded on a rock"—has used the rock as a symbol of the strength and security its insurance provides.

At the time this skyscraper was built, the Prudential Insurance Company had already erected a number of skyscrapers in the United States, the most famous of which is probably the one in Boston, Massachusetts. To Americans, the Prudential buildings scattered throughout America were the symbols of the strength of the life insurance company, and ultimately they came to embody the financial institution itself. For Chicagoans, the building hearkens back to the city's ebullient 1950s. When the building opened, Richard J. Daley had just won his first mayoral election. Daley would be mayor from 1955 to 1976, when he died while still in office. Daley gained a reputation as one of the nation's last big city mayors, and together with the Prudential building, his administration symbolized the stability of the central city. Both the mayor and the life insurance company symbolized investment in Chicago, and that made some citizens feel secure that the city did indeed have something worth investing in.

Even though much taller buildings have long since raised the Chicago skyline above the Prudential's roof, the building's 73-foot antenna makes it seem like the Prudential could still compete for the title of "Chicago's tallest."

Photo Copyright: Roger Ressmeyer/Corbis

Sears Tower

Chicago is a town that loves superlatives, and at 110 stories and 1450 feet the Sears Tower is the tallest building not only in Chicago but in all of North America. As a result, it is an absolute must-see for many visitors and residents alike. Workers carried out the construction between 1968 and 1974, and Sears Roebuck & Company, the great mail order and department store company, was headquartered there until 1995 when it moved to its corporate campus in Hoffman Estates, Illinois.

The Sears Tower features a Skydeck with views on a clear day of the neighboring states of Indiana, Wisconsin, and Michigan 40 to 50 miles away. If you make the trip be sure to prepare for your ears to pop not just once, but two or three times as you go up the elevator. In addition to spectacular views above the clouds, the Skydeck features displays on the city's history.

McCormick Place

McCormick Place, at 2301 S. Lake Shore Drive, is Chicago's central forum for trade shows and exhibitions. While many question the location of the building on the city's lakefront, no one questions the importance of the economic role that conventions and tourism play in the city. Historically, Chicago was host to a great number of national and state conventions and trade shows due to its central location and myriad rail connections. In the nineteenth century, many of these events took place in the Inter State Industrial Exposition Building, which was also located on the lakefront, where the Art Institute of Chicago building stands today.

Many Chicagoans can recount the story of the first McCormick Place, built in 1960. When it burned down in 1967, a great many groups lobbied to have the building relocated away from the lakefront, but the need to get the vital structure back up and running as quickly as possible left no time to go searching for a new location. The replacement building is a stunning and functional structure, providing 300,000 square feet of open exhibit space, with just a few columns that interrupt the display area. In 1986 the city added McCormick Place North at 450 E. 23rd Street, which features an interesting diamond-patterned exterior. Then, in 1996, McCormick Place South was added at 2301 S. King Drive. Unlike the other structures, which were made exclusively for trade shows, this building primarily hosts meetings.

The James R. Thompson Center

Completed in 1985, the James R. Thompson Center at 100 W. Randolph Street is one of Chicago's most innovative structures. The design was an unusual choice for the State of Illinois, but then-Governor Thompson lobbied hard for the structure. It was designed by Helmut Jahn, an architect from Nuremberg, Germany, who spent a year at the Illinois Institute of Technology studying under Ludwig Mies van der Rohe. Jahn designed several other buildings in Chicago, including the United Airlines Terminal at O'Hare Airport.

The central space within the center is an impressive, seventeen-story-high atrium. Around it are situated state and other government agencies, including the State of Illinois Department of Motor Vehicles (the DMV) and a post office. On the lower level of the building is a food court with a wide range of dining options and an excellent view of the large atrium just above it. One of the hidden gems within the building is the Illinois State Museum Chicago Gallery, which presents temporary exhibits that feature the art and artists of Illinois. In front of the building stands Jean Dubuffet's (1901-1985) controversial work, *Monument with Standing Beast*. One critic purportedly called the piece "Snoopy in the Blender"; another dubbed it "Pile of Dirty Snow." Love it or hate it, the sculpture draws viewers to walk around and into the space it creates.

Both the James R. Thompson Center and Dubuffet's sculpture are made more interesting by their surroundings. Part of the allure of the Thompson Center is the contrast that it creates with the nearby Daley Center, a modernist skyscraper, and the Chicago City Hall and Cook County Building, a neoclassical skyscraper. The architecture of each of these three government buildings makes a completely different impression on the viewer. Similarly, Jean Dubuffet's fiberglass sculpture is just one sample in a spectacular gallery of twentieth-century outdoor art scattered around the Loop: *Untitled Sculpture* (1967), by Pablo Picasso, is a central feature of Daley Plaza; Alexander Calder's *Flamingo* (1974) is located at the Federal Center; Marc Chagall's *The Four Seasons* (1974) stands at First National Plaza; and Joan Miró's *Chicago* (1981) is just south of W. Washington Street at Clark Street.

Jean Dubuffet's controversial Monument with Standing Beast, *in front of the James R. Thompson Center.*

333 Wacker Drive

The 333 Wacker Drive Building is one of a new generation of buildings in Chicago known primarily by their addresses, rather than by their corporate names. This particular structure is so unique that it is often even referred to as just "333." Completed in 1983, some speak of it as Chicago's first postmodern skyscraper, and though some visitors say they do not favor contemporary architecture, this elegant specimen has changed quite a few minds.

The office building has gained an international reputation as one of the most popular glass skyscrapers in the world. Americans most often recognize it after being told that it was featured in John Hughes' popular 1986 film *Ferris Buehler's Day Off*, a virtual travelogue of Chicago sites, in which Matthew Broderick's character's father has an office in the 333 building. It is located on the northeast end of Chicago's Loop, near the Orleans Bridge and the Lake Street elevated trains. Historically, this area was a center of trade in the city, and many of Chicago's oldest businesses once lined the river here.

The architectural firm hired to design 333, Kohn Pedersen Fox, had to work with a very unique site. The lot is located at the point where the main branch of the Chicago River meets the north and the south branches, creating a natural curve in the river. That curve makes the building's plot triangular, a fact the designers were able to take advantage of to appropriate a bit of the river's natural beauty for 333. This they did by constructing the building's 365-foot-wide, 36-story-tall façade of curving, green-tinted, reflective glass, from which the base of the building is distinguished by its striped marble construction. Depending on the location and angle from which it is viewed, the glass might reflect the river itself, other buildings across the way, or the sky.

This clever use of riverside location is indicative of a "river revival" taking place in Chicago, a city that once used its precious waterway as a sewer for an entire century. Like so many other cities in the twenty-first century, however, Chicago has finally embraced the river for its aesthetic and recreational promise. Many people now like to take one of the architectural tours offered in the city, and those who do are justifiably awed by the view from the river of the gargantuan Merchandise Mart, the unusual towers of Marina City, and especially by the river's reflection in 333.

Bank One
Corporate Center

Looking up from almost any point within Chicago's Loop, the viewer sees interesting juxtapositions. The Bank One Corporate Center at 131 S. Dearborn Street, for example, is a post-modern structure completed by Ricardo Bofill Arquitectura in 2003, making it one of the newest skyscrapers in the city. It is flanked by two much older buildings, though: the Marquette Building, of the first school of Chicago architecture, and the Everett McKinley Dirksen Building, one of Ludwig Mies van der Rohe's modernist structures from the second school of Chicago architecture. Thankfully, the old and the new don't seem to clash at all. Rather, a dialogue between the very different buildings is created by the corporate center's façade of highly reflective glass, which also gives it its slick-looking design.

The 39-story building was erected as the corporate offices of Bank One Corporation. In 2005, the merger between Bank One and JPMorgan Chase created JPMorgan Chase & Co., now a banking leader with assets of over $1 trillion and operations in over 50 countries. The corporate center in Chicago houses the firm's retail financial services and commercial banking headquarters, while corporate headquarters are in New York. In a great spirit of optimism about its future here, the company placed a gilded reproduction of the *Winged Victory of Samothrace*—one of the world's most famous sculptures and a classic symbol of triumph—at the glass entry on Dearborn Street.

Chicago Moves: By Water, Earth, and Air

Lake Michigan and the Chicago River

The earliest travelers to the area that would become known as Chicago often arrived by way of Lake Michigan. Native Americans made their way in canoes; French voyagers traveled down from Canada to trade; and, in time, some New England Yankees would arrive in schooners. These first visitors were greeted at the mouth of the Chicago River by a large sandbar that blocked the entrance to the river, forcing them to portage their canoes at this point.

Both Lake Michigan and the Chicago River contributed to Chicago's rise as a major national transportation hub. In its early history, the city was a crucial connecting point between the Great Lakes and the Mississippi River Valley, connecting New York to New Orleans right through its shores. Early settlers utilized the strategically located port for commerce, reserving only a portion of the lakefront as "open, clear and free" land intended for citizens' enjoyment and refreshment. As Chicago began its rapid growth into a powerful nineteenth-century industrial city, the Army Corps of Engineers built a breakwater and dredged the river. Industrialism turned the city into a great coal-belcher, and for a while factories and other waste-makers dumped their refuse directly into these precious bodies of water.

The city has become a shining example of the meeting of old and new economies, and is now home to many high-tech and cutting-edge industries that are less dependent on—and less polluting of—local water supplies. With the development of air, rail, and highway systems, the waterways became less crucial to the transportation industry as well. Now, the lake is appreciated primarily for its beauty and recreational usefulness. Many locals boat on the river, fish in its waters, and stroll along its formerly industrialized shores. The lakefront is the site of a variety of events and festivals, including the city's jazz, blues, and gospel music festivals; the Taste of Chicago, an event that attracts millions of visitors each July to come taste the offerings of Chicago's restaurants; a free summer music series; and Venetian Night, on which viewers line the shore to watch boats sparkling with lights parade along the water. Chicago's Fourth of July fireworks show is also held on the lakefront.

Visitors from all around the world are no longer greeted at the shores of Lake Michigan by a pesky sandbar, but by the sprawling metropolis of Chicago that towers above it. "Open, clear and free" land is still provided by Grant Park and Millennium Park, which dominate the lakefront at the city center. And Chicago's great museums, including the Art Institute of Chicago, the Field Museum, the Shedd Aquarium, and the Adler Planetarium, stand ready to receive guests nearby. Many visitors take architectural-themed boat tours on the Chicago River, or pleasure cruises on Lake Michigan. These activities provide welcome recreation, as well as a glimpse into the city's earliest history, making them well worth the expense.

View of the city from Lake Michigan.

Previous page: View of Chicago Harbor from Shedd Aquarium.

Pioneer Chicago and Defense

The Michigan Avenue Bridge was constructed in the 1920s over the Chicago River, near the point where the river enters Lake Michigan, the site of Chicago's earliest settlement. Native Americans recognized the location's favored position to portage between the Great Lakes and the Mississippi River watershed, and it is likely that many of them passed through this location on their travels between Lake Michigan and the Chicago River. Later, in 1673, French missionary Jacques Marquette and French-Canadian explorer Louis Jolliet passed through the area and noted its unique location as well. The site soon became known as "Checaugou," a name believed to have come from the Potawatomi word for a "wild onion" that grew in the low, swampy area.

Although the city's earliest history has been largely erased over time, the Michigan Avenue Bridge features four historic bas-reliefs by New York-born Henry Hering, installed in 1928. Hering studied at the Art Students League in New York and the *Ecoles des Beaux Arts* in Paris, and often assisted one of the most famous nineteenth-century sculptors, Augustus Saint-Gaudens.

In *Pioneer Chicago* the artist captures how, in a single century, Chicago grew from a small settlement of a few people to one of the largest metropolises in the world. Hering's depiction of pioneer Chicago is certainly idealized, but it is a good reminder of those who laid the foundation for the modern city on these very shores.

With the Louisiana Purchase of 1803, the United States built Fort Dearborn near this spot as well. Its appearance underlined the tension that

Pioneer Chicago, *depicting the city's early settlers.*

Defense, *depicting the Battle of Chicago (locally known as the Fort Dearborn Massacre) in the War of 1812.*

existed between the U.S. Army and the native inhabitants, as well as the geographic importance of this site to the budding nation and its potential as a crucial transportation link in the country.

During the War of 1812, fought between the United States and Great Britain, the allies of each side included various Native American tribes, and so the troops at Fort Dearborn feared attack by local Native Americans allied with Britain. On August 13, 1812, American troops finally abandoned the fort and began to move south along Lake Michigan toward Fort Detroit The group, which included dozens of American soldiers and their supporters, was attacked and killed not far from the Michigan Avenue Bridge. Within the scope of the War of 1812, this event is known as the Battle of Chicago. Locally, it is known as the

Fort Dearborn Massacre. Hering's most dynamic relief, entitled *Defense*, has this battle as its historical theme. The sculpture forces one to look over the shoulder of an army officer embroiled in battle with a Native American, thus bringing the viewer right into the fight.

Looking around at the site today, it is hard to believe that Chicago's earliest history is marked by the often-bloody conflicts between Native Americans and the new arrivals, or to envision the sprawling metropolis as swampy land on the sandy shores of Lake Michigan. The Hering sculptures, placed in such a prominent and appropriate location, provide this unique perspective that helps passers-by to link the modern location with the historic themes that would otherwise be obscured by time.

Quincy Station

Few sights or sounds in Chicago are as evocative of the past as the elevated trains. Quincy Station, one of the last remaining original Loop stations, is the symbol of Chicago's elevated railway system. Restored to its 1897 appearance by the city, the station does not have elevators or escalators, but features the original fare collection booths and wooden advertisement cases with Victorian-era advertisements.

The elevated train system is the best remaining evidence of just how crowded Chicago was in the 1890s. Hoping to alleviate the crowding, entrepreneurs invested money and gathered political support for the construction of a united elevated rail system. In a city in which so many people—and animals—vied for use of the streets, near gridlock was not an uncommon occurrence. Not to mention the facts that public transportation had only aided the expansion of the city, and that the city had recently annexed a huge area to its jurisdiction. This brought even more people in to work inside Chicago's "Loop," as Chicagoans called the area served by the cable cars, which traveled in a loop that defined the city center.

The Loop once traveled by the cable cars is now followed (more or less) by the city's elevated lines, and the system has become a part of the Chicago Transit Authority, the second-largest transit system in the country. There are around 1,150 rapid transit cars in the system, making most of Chicago's attractions seem just a step away from any point in the city.

North Avenue Beach

Each of the many beaches along the city's miles of lakefront has its own style and reputation and is worthy of investigation. Oak Street Beach, for example, is a fashionable site for sunbathing. North Avenue Beach, on the other hand, is geared toward active recreation, and that's made it one of Chicago's most popular beaches. Although the beach looks like a "natural" landscape, the city actually created the beaches and parkland in the early twentieth century through the use of landfill. The result is an incredibly popular space within the city limits of which residents are justifiably proud.

The City of Chicago works hard to manage the variety of facilities and activities along the lakefront. Particularly in the summer months, visitors will find Chicagoans making considerable use of the bike path for jogging, biking, rollerblading, and other relatively high-speed activities. Others take advantage of the beach volleyball courts, an outdoor fitness center with weight lifting, and a roller hockey rink, as well as designated places for dogs to swim and cars to park along the lakefront. Each summer a great number of lifeguards are hired, and many Chicagoans take sailing lessons from the park district. North Avenue Beach features a beach house that has concessions and restrooms, as well as a restaurant called Castaways that makes this beach in particular a fantastic spot even for those who would rather people-watch than be active.

Union Station

Since 1848, when the first railroad train came chugging into Chicago, the Midwestern city has become the rail hub of the entire nation. Although train travel no longer occupies a central place in America's transportation system, visitors are often surprised by the number of trains in and around Chicago. It is still possible to travel around the United States and Canada via rail, and Chicago remains the national rail hub of Amtrak, the United States' national passenger line provider. In addition, great numbers of daily commuters make their way in and out of the city by rail on Metra, the regional provider.

Chicago's Union Station was one of the last great railroad stations built in the United States. It was envisioned by Daniel Burnham and Edward

Bennett in their 1909 Plan for Chicago, which set out a bold vision for the development of many of the city's important civic elements. The plan paid particular attention to residents' transportation needs and established the central role of the lakefront, in particular Grant Park, the Cook County Building and City Hall, and Union Station. The plan was adopted by the city of Chicago and the station was completed in 1925. Like many of Chicago's buildings, the neoclassical exterior was built to massive proportions, but the main waiting area has the power to captivate and draw visitors into the impressive interior. The station was significantly renovated in the early 1990s, and is now complete with ticket agent windows, newsstands, and an extensive food court and waiting area.

Although most Americans no longer travel by rail, many Chicagoans still choose to take the train for work and pleasure. In the summertime, it is a great joy to ride by rail to the evening concerts at the Ravinia Festival in Highland Park, Illinois. Any time of year is a good time to take the train to nearby communities such as Joliet or Naperville, or to Illinois' state capital in Springfield, which has excellent rail service and a station at the city center that is within walking distance of a number of the famed Lincoln sites.

The Michigan Avenue Bridge

The Michigan Avenue Bridge is arguably the most spectacular bridge in the city. Completed in 1920, it became the first double-deck trunnion bascule bridge ever built, and was hailed as a wonder for both its beauty and engineering. It was designed by architect Edward Bennett (also responsible for Buckingham Fountain in the city's Grant Park) and engineered by Hugh Young. On either end of the bridge are bas-reliefs by sculptor Henry Hering depicting historical subjects, including Chicago pioneers and the Battle of Chicago from the War of 1812. Visitors to the city often remark on the bridge's spectacular prospect of the river and view of Lake Michigan to the east, though locals rarely notice it at all.

The bascule bridge uses a system of counterweights, gears, and motors to rotate the sides of the bridge up and back. The tremendous weight of the span is balanced by the counterweights, which are located below the roadway of the bridge. The Michigan Avenue Bridge features two leaves, each weighing around 3,340 tons and sheathed by the bridge's attractive neoclassical elements. The bridge's operator is situated in a control room with the mechanisms for raising and lowering the spans. The raising and lowering process involves multiple steps, including closing traffic gates and assuring that all pedestrian and vehicle traffic is clear.

The bridge spans the earliest inhabited area of the city near the mouth of the Chicago River. Its construction promoted the development of North Michigan Avenue, as well as the creation of one of the most impressive intersections in the city. It also opened up direct access to the area north of the river, and that area features some of the grandest buildings from the era of the bridge's construction, including two of Chicago's iconic structures, the Wrigley Building and Tribune Tower. Wrigley, as most Americans know, gained his fame and fortune for his chewing gum and became the noted owner of the Chicago Cubs baseball team. Lesser known is the Tribune Company, which operates a major Chicago newspaper and one of the city's great radio stations, WGN.

Residents in Chicago tend to divide themselves out along the river's contours. The division between Northsiders, Southsiders, and Westsiders often dictates allegiances to the city's much beloved and revered professional baseball teams. Northsiders tend to declare their allegiance to the Chicago Cubs of Major League Baseball's National League. The south side more often favors the American League's Chicago White Socks. The river divides the city in other ways as well, most notably by socio-economic status. Northsiders are commonly portrayed as "yuppies," young urban professionals, while the south side is home to the working class. All of these divisions tend to be generalities, of course, but they show the great influence that Chicago's geography and especially the Chicago River have on the city's residents.

Route 66/Michigan Avenue

On Adams Street just off Michigan Avenue in Chicago stands a sign marking the start of Route 66, a much-beloved symbol of freedom and mobility in the United States. After Congress passed legislation for the national road's construction in 1925, workers began cutting through the entire American Southwest to link Chicago and Los Angeles. The 2,400-mile-long "mother road" marked the ascent of the automobile in America, offering people the ability to drive great distances at heretofore never-conceived-of speed.

A great many people enjoyed not just its speed and freedom, but the many roadside attractions that dotted the route, such as the 170-foot-high World's Largest Catsup Bottle in Collinsville, Illinois. In fact, the road was so popular at one time that it became an integral element of American pop culture. Bobby Troup wrote a song in 1946 called *Route 66* that Nat King Cole and many other musicians have recorded. The road was also immortalized in a television program called *Route 66*. Beginning in 1960, it ran for three years and featured two characters, Todd Stiles and Buzz Murdock, who traveled the road in a 1960 Corvette.

Some argue that Route 66's popularity was the first sign of its own demise. It was an indication that automobile travel would necessarily become a way of life in America—which meant that it would require constant improvement. By the 1950s, the United States was already looking forward to a more up-to-date highway system: President Dwight D. Eisenhower saw the strategic benefit of a new system of divided highways, which were both faster and safer than two-lane roads, and he soon signed the Federal Aid Highway Act of 1956 to provide funds for the national interstate and defense highway system. By 1970, nearly all segments of the original Route 66 had been replaced by modern four-lane highways.

Nevertheless, segments of Route 66 are still there, and they still feature a great number of period diners and motels. Many travelers follow the route today just to feel the sense of adventure that the old two-lane road once conjured in the American soul. Others just prefer its small scale, and still others prefer to know they'll have the option of resting off-road beside the world's largest ball of twine or of sleeping the night in a motel of concrete teepees. Adventurers in Illinois should be sure to stop for a bite at the Dixie Truckers Home in McLean, one of the oldest and best truck stops in the state, or at the Ariston Café in Litchfield—or at both. Those headed further west should note that some people argue that the most charming section of Route 66 is to be found not in Illinois, but New Mexico, where the El Rancho hotel is located. Built by the brother of director D. W. Griffith, the hotel features rooms named after movie stars who have stayed there, including John Wayne and Ronald Reagan.

Burnham Harbor

With 307 miles of length and 118 miles of width, Lake Michigan provides a vast area to explore. It has a maximum depth of 925 feet, and filling it in is a wide array of marine life, including salmon, trout, and yellow perch. That is the reason why Chicagoans are so fond of sailing and other water activities—and why Burnham Harbor is one of the most popular sites for setting out. It is located in the city's new Museum Campus area, just to the south of the John G. Shedd Aquarium and the Field Museum of Natural History. The harbor is named in honor of Daniel Hudson Burnham, the architect and planner whose work transformed Chicago's lakefront. It is largely because of Burnham's vision that visitors to Burnham Harbor or Chicago Harbor to the north find the lakefront as enjoyable an experience as they do.

After his work on the World's Columbian Exposition of 1893, Burnham announced that the next great work of Chicago should be the lakefront, and he began working closely with architect Edward Bennett to publish their 1909 Plan for Chicago. The plan was a comprehensive one that focused on the city center and its transportation system and provided for the future growth and progress of the metropolis, guaranteeing future generations a practical as well as an elegant metropolitan area. For the lakefront, Burnham and Bennett conceptualized a new shoreline that would stretch from Evanston to the Indiana state line and feature a whole series of lagoons, harbors, and park areas. These man-made features all terminated at a large yacht harbor—Chicago Harbor—that the architects placed in Grant Park in the center of the Chicago lakefront.

Of the many harbors created and operated by the Chicago Park District, Burnham Harbor is the most sheltered. It is home to the Burnham Park Yacht Club, which offers sailing, educational, and social activities, as well as 1,120 docks and other amenities, including a fuel dock, ship supply store, and launch ramp.

Chicago Gathers: Out of Many Neighborhoods, One City

Old Saint Patrick's Church

Old Saint Patrick's Church, at 718 W. Adams Street, is the oldest standing neighborhood parish of the Chicago Irish. The church's history goes back to 1846, when the parish was founded, but the present structure was completed in 1856. In the nineteenth century, Chicago's immigrant neighborhoods commonly centered around a religious institution. For the droves of new Irish immigrants driven out of Ireland by the Great Potato Famine (1846-1849), the Young Ireland Rebellion (1848), and general economic hardship, Saint Patrick's became the place to pray for a hopeful future as much as to meet other people from "the old country."

From 1912 to 1922, Thomas O'Shaughnessy created a masterpiece of Irish ecclesiastical art within Saint Patrick's, transforming the church into the best example of Celtic Revival art in America. O'Shaughnessy studied stained glass and stenciling at the School of the Art Institute of Chicago, and spent a good portion of his career educating the public about the art of Ireland. From without, his influence can be seen in the Celtic cross on the side of the building. Within, he drew inspiration for his stained glass windows from the four New Testament Gospels illustrations in the fantastic eighth-century illuminated manuscript, *The Book of Kells*. (*The Book of Kells* is a top tourist attraction in Dublin, Ireland, where it is housed in the library of Trinity College.)

Today, Celtic art has become an international style, but Chicago's Old Saint Patrick's Church has a unique claim to the roots of this influence on the modern world. Saint Patrick's was purportedly down to only four members in recent years, but has since become reinvigorated and is part of the revitalization of downtown Chicago. Its annual St. Patrick's "World's Largest Block Party" has become one of the most festive summer events in the city.

Previous page: Sunrise over Chicago skyline.

Holy Name Cathedral

At 735 N. State Street stands one of the city's noblest landmarks. Holy Name Cathedral hearkens back to Chicago's early history. The first church on the site, the Chapel of the Holy Name of the University of St. Mary of the Lake, was constructed in 1846 and rebuilt as Holy Name Parish in 1854. After the Great Chicago Fire of 1871 destroyed the parish church, Brooklyn architect Patrick C. Keeley began rebuilding on the site—not a chapel, not a parish, but a glorious cathedral. He designed it in the Gothic Revival style and built it of locally quarried Lemont limestone, which lends the structure a quiet dignity.

Since its completion in 1875, Holy Name Cathedral has been significantly modified and expanded several times. Some visitors are taken aback by the unexpectedly modern interior, which was significantly remodeled in 1969. It features a number of interesting elements, including a massive organ that was handmade at the world-renowned workshops of Flentrop Orgelbouw in Zaandam, Holland. The cathedral has served as the seat of several bishops and cardinals, and visitors can see evidence of that fact if they just look up into the rafters, where all the galeros—the traditional broad-brimmed, red cardinal's hat—of Holy Name's cardinals hang. Among them are the galeros worn by Archbishops Mundelein, Stritch, and Meyer. The latest hat belonged to Cardinal Bernardin, a well-loved man who worked hard to reach out to other faith communities. Bernardin fought a very publicized battle with cancer, during which Chicagoans marvelled at the great dignity with which he managed to carry himself even into death.

In a major event for the Roman Catholic faithful of the city, Pope John Paul II visited the cathedral on his 1979 trip to Chicago, during which he also celebrated mass with hundreds of thousands in Grant Park. In more recent years, Chicago's Roman Catholic church has undergone significant change. While a large number of Irish, Polish, and other European immigrants' descendants continue on as members, the face of the church has been transformed by recent immigrations from Mexico, Central America, Vietnam, and Africa. Reflecting national trends, Chicago's Catholics have also had to contend with budget deficits, decaying infrastructure, and even shrinking mass attendance in many parishes. Despite these problems, Holy Name Cathedral continues to play a central role in the city. It is still the seat of Chicago's archbishops, and the gorgeous edifice still beckons passersby into its calm, quiet interior, a refuge from the sometimes frenetic activity of the world outside.

פתחו לי שערי צדק אבא בם אודה יה

OPEN FOR ME THE GATES OF RIGHTEOUSNESS,
THAT I MAY ENTER THROUGH THEM, TO PRAISE THE LORD.

Pilgrim Baptist Church

The Pilgrim Baptist Church building was originally home to Kehilath Anshe Ma'ariv ("Community of the People of the West," abbreviated KAM) Synagogue. Noted Chicago architects Dankmar Adler and Louis Sullivan designed the synagogue at 3301 S. Indiana Avenue between 1890 and 1891 for Chicago's oldest Jewish congregation, which dated back to 1847.

Interestingly, Adler's father was rabbi of the community from 1861 to 1883. Adler didn't get the job just because he was the rabbi's son, though. He and Sullivan had gained international fame for the Auditorium Building at 430 S. Michigan Avenue, constructed between 1887 and 1889. The 4,300-seat theater in the building became the home of Chicago's operatic and symphonic events, and the success of the project contributed significantly to the recognition of Adler's acoustical skill. The congregation specifically desired an acoustically superior interior for their new home, hence Adler and his partner seemed the top choice.

Due to changes in neighborhood demographics, the KAM Synagogue was rededicated as Pilgrim Baptist Church in 1926. It soon gained international recognition for the work of Dr. Thomas Dorsey, who became world-renowned as the originator of gospel music while serving as the church's musical director. His most famous song is probably *Precious Lord*, which he wrote while mourning his first wife after she died in childbirth in 1932. His music has been performed internationally and his choirs—which featured Mahalia Jackson, one of the city's greatest gospel singers, as a member—gained great acclaim.

For a while, the congregation of Pilgrim Baptist stood at the center of a great artistic and commercial enterprise in Chicago's African-American community. To this day, the church building still embodies the history and vibrancy of this area, Chicago's near south side. The church serves mostly low-income families, though, and despite the fact that the neighborhood is undergoing gentrification, the building is presently in need of extensive renovation and the congregation does not have the resources to undertake the project. Nevertheless, Pilgrim Baptist continues to reach out to the community in a number of ways, including programs offered to local youths and the elderly.

First Presbyterian Church

First Presbyterian Church in Lake View is another fine example of church architecture in Chicago. It was erected in 1888 at 716 W. Addison Street by the architectural team of Daniel H. Burnham and John Wellborn Root. It features a high-pitched roof with an octagonal tower and a wooden frame construction, which was banned within the city limits after the fire of 1871. The original church cost around $13,000 to build, but just one decade later the congregation had grown so much that expansion was necessary.

At the time of its construction, the church was located in the Lake View Township, a small community outside Chicago that featured a number of small farms and little country estates. The area gained a reputation for its greenhouses, and at one time was the nation's largest shipper of celery. The year following the church's construction, Chicagoans voted Lake View and other areas into the city, thereby adding 125 square miles to Chicago's jurisdiction. In return, the annexed areas gained improved city services. Because of its favored location along the lake, Lake View quickly became a desirable residential area. Today it is near the north-side communities of Uptown and Ravenswood, both interesting neighborhoods to take an afternoon stroll in.

Throughout its history, First Presbyterian's congregation has been responsive to the needs of the surrounding community. In its early history, the congregation taught English to immigrants. Today it provides programs for at-risk youth and serves hot lunches to neighborhood senior citizens.

Fourth Presbyterian Church

Just as the University of Chicago's Gothic Revival campus created a kind of sacred educational space on Chicago's south side, the Gothic Revival-style Fourth Presbyterian Church at 866 N. Michigan Avenue is a site of calm reflection downtown. Erected just before the Michigan Avenue building boom of the the 1920s, Fourth Pres (as it is known locally) quickly attracted members from all around the Chicago area. Its sanctuary features fine wood appointments, elegant stained glass windows, and the largest— and some would argue the finest—organ in the city. The instrument itself is an Aeolian Skinner Organ from 1971, but some of its pipe work dates back to 1914. It is a significant feature of the church's worship services, renowned for their inspiring music. The congregation also offers a number of noontime concerts during the week.

In the last decade, Michigan Avenue underwent a major building boom that turned the street into Chicago's largest, most fashionable retail area. While the church has been dwarfed by the new construction, its value to the community has in some ways actually been intensified: the more things change, the more potently symbolic Fourth Pres becomes of an earlier time, when the little church was still the neighborhood's major anchor.

Holy Trinity Russian Orthodox Cathedral

The city's northwest side is notable for Humboldt Park and the number of churches in the area. Holy Trinity, however, is unique as a symbol of immigrants bringing their own culture and traditions with them to their new homelands. Located at 1121 N. Leavitt Street, the church's neighborhood was inhabited by Germans, Poles, Scandinavians, and Italians at the time of its construction. Russian immigrants were largely responsible for its construction, though, and even Czar Nicholas II of Russia facilitated the work with a donation of $4,000.

The community hired Chicago architect Louis H. Sullivan—now revered as one of the nation's greatest architects—to design an intimate little church, and Sullivan worked on the project for four years, between 1899 and 1903. Sullivan built a traditional Eastern Orthodox church in the Byzantine style. For those familiar primarily with Western Christianity, the church's tower and octagonal dome are like an otherworldly presence in the city. On the inside, the iconostasis—a screen decorated with golden icons—divides the sanctuary from the nave and creates a division between the priest and the congregation. The church's many icons are richly decorated themselves, as is the Eastern tradition, endowing them with the power to communicate the presence of a mysterious, sacred realm.

Chicago Marvels: Great Events that Shaped the City

Statue of the Republic

The noted nineteenth-century sculptor Daniel Chester French created the *Statue of the Republic* for Chicago's 1893 World's Columbian Exposition. Celebrating the 400th anniversary of Columbus' arrival in America, the fair's host had to meet exceedingly high expectations, especially after the precedent set by the 1889 Paris Exposition, which featured the Eiffel Tower. After Chicago beat out New York and Washington, D.C. for the right to host the fair, the city felt the pressure of the world's expectations even more.

But there was never any reason to worry. Chicago met and even exceeded the world's expectations, emerging through this singular event as the metropolis of the Midwest. In fact, the exposition marked a watershed moment not just in the history of Chicago, but of the whole nation. It was an enormous cultural success, and it demonstrated to the world that the still-young United States—and the still younger Chicago—could pull off a major world event. (It also proved to be a big moneymaker, which was naturally of great importance to its investors.) Because the whole process was so well organized, the event became a model for future urban planning as well as artistic achievement.

Because most of the 1893 exposition was created out of temporary materials, there remain few physical reminders of the excitement—but Daniel Chester French's statue is one of the few. French was one of the great sculptors of his age and gained renown for such works as the Lincoln Memorial in Washington, D.C. His *Statue of the Republic*, made out of plaster staff over a metal frame, was perfectly executed for its purpose at the exhibition. The 72-foot-tall allegorical Republic was prominently placed in the exposition's vaunted Court of Honor, where it served as a powerful embodiment of the sense of progress that pervaded the fair.

Unfortunately, the original sculpture was destroyed by a fire in 1896. However, the replica that visitors see today in Jackson Park is also the work of Daniel Chester French. Together with architect Henry Bacon, French created the 24-foot replica and pedestal for the 25th anniversary of the exposition and the 100th birthday of the entry of the State of Illinois into the United States in 1918. The funds for the work were the last $48,000 remaining from the fair's foundation. When the foundation disbanded in 1915, it turned the money over to the Ferguson Monument Fund of the Art Institute of Chicago to create a statue commemorating the exhibition.

The Republic—or "the Golden Lady," as she is popularly known—depicts a woman in a long, flowing robe and breastplate with her arms held above her head. In her right hand are a globe and an eagle—the fair's emblems; in her left she holds a staff with a laurel. In 1992, the statue underwent a thorough restoration, and now it is an even shinier and more spectacular symbol of the exciting days in which it was born.

Previous page: View of Anish Kapoor's sculpture Cloud Gate *from below.*

The Museum of Science and Industry

Like the *Statue of the Republic*, the Museum of Science and Industry building at S. Lake Shore Drive and E. 57th Street offers a glimpse of the glory of the World's Columbian Exposition. It was originally built as the Palace of Fine Arts, which was to display works of art from around the world at the fair, and so exhibition planners thought it best to construct the building of fireproof material. Since most exhibition buildings were constructed of temporary materials, the museum is now the only building that remains from the fair in Jackson Park.

As were all the exhibition buildings, the Palace of Fine Arts building was constructed in the neoclassical style. The original structure was designed by Charles B. Atwood in 1893, but the building has undergone significant reconstruction and expansion since it opened. Looking at the

Museum of Science and Industry today, one can almost imagine the legendary "White City" created by all those glorious white structures. After the World's Columbian Exposition, the building housed the Field Museum of Natural History. When that institution moved into another Burnham-designed neoclassical structure in Grant Park in 1920, it left the building a shell of its former self. In the next couple of decades, the building was remodeled and the exterior redone in marble and limestone.

Today, the building belongs to the Museum of

Science and Industry and houses some of the most beloved attractions in the city. "Take Flight" takes visitors inside a 727 jetliner, for instance, and not only history buffs think the German *U-505* submarine, which was captured by the United States Navy during World War II, is really cool. The Coal Mine exhibit is so realistic that at least one visitor commented on how fortunate the museum was to be built on top of a coal mine! In 1998, the museum added an interesting underground entrance, which featured a Silver Streak, the famous 1930s locomotive.

The Art Institute of Chicago

The Art Institute of Chicago, on Michigan Avenue at Adams Street, is one of Chicago's most visited sites and one of the world's greatest art museums. Its Michigan Avenue entrance is the oldest part of the building, featuring a pair of lions on guard at the institute since 1894. Created by sculptor Edward Kemeys, the pair has served as unofficial representatives of the city—a great honor in a city famous for its many impressive outdoor sculptures. Kemeys drew inspiration from lions that had been sculpted out of temporary material for the World's Columbian Exposition. Although massive and impressive on their own, they often dress up for important occasions, including after Thanksgiving, when their festive wreathing shows their holiday cheer.

Today, visitors come to Grant Park with little thought of its role in the great exposition of 1893, but this was actually the proposed site of the fair. In fact, the Art Institute of Chicago served as an auxiliary site for the events. It staged the World's Columbian Exposition's congresses, which were scholarly presentations on a variety of topics such as photography, history, and world religion. After the congresses concluded, the Art Institute of Chicago took control of the building.

The museum has been on the forefront of research and interpretation for several decades. One of its most renowned innovations was the founding of the School of the Art Institute, which trains many students in both the applied arts and in fields such as historic preservation. The museum features a number of high-profile exhibits each year in addition to its permanent collection of French Impressionist, Asian, African, Amerindian, and American art. Many visitors come just to see much-loved works in the permanent collections, such as Marc Chagall's compelling stained glass work *American Windows*, Georges Seurat's *A Sunday Afternoon on the Island of La Grande Jatte*, and Grant Wood's often parodied *American Gothic*.

The museum also features remnants from Chicago's architectural past. Without a doubt, the most imposing are the Entrance Arch and Trading Room from Adler and Sullivan's 1893 Chicago Stock Exchange Building, demolished in 1972. Today, many visitors pass the Art Institute's quiet, sunken garden at Monroe Street and Columbus Drive without even noticing the Entrance Arch, standing like a glorious ruin in the midst of the green landscaping. The Trading Room was incorporated into an addition constructed in 1977. It features the marvelous capitals, windows, and stenciling that made the original structure so spectacular. Other fragments of the building are displayed at the top of the grand staircase leading up to the institute's main entrance on Michigan Avenue.

The original entrance arch from the Chicago Stock Exchange building, on display for all in the institute's garden at Monroe Street and Columbus Drive.

Located just north of the Michigan Avenue entrance is the Stanley McCormick Memorial Court, a surprisingly quiet haven in the midst of the bustling city. The court features sculptures by Henry Moore and Alexander Calder, as well as a great deal of plant life. The area has a central lawn and features ornamental grasses, native honey locust trees, and very often seasonal plantings that make visiting the area a joy almost any time of year. The Robert Allerton Building, one of the museum's many additions, serves as the backdrop to this hidden garden, and the Crown Fountain in Millennium Park can be seen when looking north from the court.

"Large Interior Form" by Henry Moore, 1982.

Christopher Columbus Statue

The Christopher Columbus Statue, located on the southern end of Grant Park, is a distinctive reminder of Chicago—and the world—in the 1930s. Cast by Carlo Brioschi, the larger-than-life Columbus stands on a large pedestal featuring "fascis," bound elm rods with axe heads that symbolized Roman imperial power—and, at the time of the statue's dedication, the Italian fascist movement of Benito Mussolini. The Columbus Monument Committee paid for the statue and organized the dedication, to which they invited the charismatic figure Italo Balbo, a regional Italian political leader who had allied himself with Mussolini. Balbo made quite an entrance to the city: he led an air squadron of state-of-the art Savoia-Marchetti SM.55X flying boats from Italy to Chicago by way of New York, landing in Chicago on July 15, 1933 in one of the great early feats of aviation. The city recognized this event with the dedication of Balbo Avenue, which runs through Grant Park.

Average Chicagoans don't think of Italian fascism every time they pass the Columbus Statue, though. Rather, it casts a backward glance to Chicago's most famous fair, the World's Columbian Exposition of 1893, which marked 400 years of civilization in the New World. Those a bit more "in the know" recognize the statue as a throwback to the Century of Progress Fair that celebrated 100 years of Chicago's incorporation as a city, during which the statue was dedicated.

Symphony Center
(formerly Orchestra Hall)

The World's Columbian Exposition of 1893 convinced the world of Chicago's cultural potential. In the decades following the expo, therefore, a great number of cultural institutions built permanent homes in the city, many of which were within or around Grant Park. This is decidedly the case for Symphony Center (originally called Orchestra Hall), located just across from Grant Park at 220 S. Michigan Avenue.

Early in the orchestra's history, a number of Chicago businessmen succeeded in convincing New York conductor Theodore Thomas to become the Chicago Orchestra's first conductor. Even though the orchestra held its first performance in the Auditorium Theater in 1891, it had no proper home at that time, and so was forced to continue practicing in a number of locations. Thomas would guide the orchestra through its first few years, but he died just weeks after the dedication of the new Orchestra Hall in 1905. Frederick Stock succeeded Thomas and continued to uphold the famously high standards of the orchestra that have become its hallmark.

Architect Daniel H. Burnham long lobbied for a permanent home for the orchestra, and eventually not only donated the land on which the hall was built, but also provided the architectural plans for the building. The Neo-Georgian façade he gave it has long been an icon on Michigan Avenue. Its red brick is accented by limestone lintels, and three giant, arched windows on the second story feature Georgian fanlights. The original name of the building, Theodore Thomas Orchestra Hall, can still be seen on the façade. The building has undergone a number of significant renovations. The most recent, in 1997, created a complex with educational space, administrative offices, and a restaurant.

The Field Museum of Natural History

The Field Museum of Natural History, opened in 1894 as the Columbian Museum of Chicago, is one of the world's great natural history museums. It was originally located in the Palace of Fine Arts building (now home to The Museum of Science and Industry) in Jackson Park, but as soon as the funds became available, the museum constructed its current home in Grant Park on the city's lakefront. It is now a central feature of the 57-acre park called the "Museum Campus," also the site of the Shedd Aquarium and Adler Planetarium.

As is clear from its façade, the museum was designed in the neoclassical style. The massive proportions of its Classical elements, such as the enormous columns at the entrance, are indicative of its 20th-century construction. Inside, the museum boasts a vast collection that includes examples of animals, plants, rocks, fossils, and even entire ecosystems, some of which date back to the World's Columbian Exposition of 1893. Visitors enjoy every possible variety of exhibit, from blockbuster displays to quiet corners of discovery. Particularly popular permanent exhibits include the Pawnee lodge and the Egyptian exhibit, which includes a real Egyptian tomb.

Still, no display is more popular than the one that the Field Museum of Natural History proudly announces as "the world's largest, most complete, and best preserved Tyrannosaurus rex." First displayed to the public in 2000, Sue (as she is affectionately called) is a star of the museum's collection. The dinosaur is named after Sue Hendrickson, who unearthed the fossilized remains in South Dakota in 1990. In a highly publicized transaction, the Field Museum gathered millions of dollars from major corporations and private individuals in order to acquire the spectacular remains.

Their eagerness to get hold of them stemmed from several reasons: At 13 feet high and 42 feet long, Sue was a ready icon for the institution and its elite collections. As the most complete set of skeletal remains known to exist, the 67-million-year-old bones also provided a great deal of very useful information for the research mission of the Field Museum. For example, the skeleton is in such a high state of preservation that it is possible to see where muscles and tendons rested and attached to the bones. And of course, a giant dinosaur skeleton named Sue was bound to attract more visitors to the museum.

Dramatically displayed within the Field Museum's main exhibition hall, Sue's bones are artfully positioned to appear as if the T-Rex were moving through the space. Many visitors do not realize that the original skull—which is 5 feet long—is too heavy for the frame and so is not the head attached to Sue's body. It is on display nearby, however, in a special exhibit devoted to Sue. Those thinking of passing up the opportunity to come see Chicago's famous T-Rex should think again: Many of the rearticulated bones on display elsewhere are reproductions cast in plastic. Sue may be the first (and only) *real specimen* many people ever see.

Pages 90–91: Sue, the world's largest, most complete, best-preserved Tyrannosaurus Rex, on display at the Field Museum. She weighed 7 tons while alive!

Daphne Garden

Chicago takes very seriously its motto, *Urbs in Horto*, "city in a garden." It has a long history as a leader in park development, and is always looking for new ways to freshen up its landscape. In the last decade, the city has reinvested in its parks and redefined their use within the metropolis, particularly in the new combination of nature and the visual arts. There have been some phenomenally successful programs, such as the glass-blower Dale Chihuly's display in Garfield Park Conservatory. Part of the success of this exhibit was the simple—but ingenious—idea to display glass works of art inside a glass conservatory.

Another innovative project undertaken by the Chicago Park District is the Summer 2004–Winter 2005 Art in the Park program, of which Daphne Garden was born. The program brought together 24 artists to design 24 gardens along a 26-mile-long stretch of Chicago's boulevard system. Their plants, sculptures, and other artistically arranged creative elements are now to be found in Grant Park, Douglas Park, Lincoln Park, Washington Park, and Washington Square Park, among others.

On the south end of Grant Park, near Roosevelt Road and Michigan Avenue, Chicago artist Dessa Kirk used parts from a disassembled Cadillac to create lilies, which were in turn assembled to create the mythical Greek figure Daphne. The myth of Daphne tells of a young woman whose father turned her into a laurel tree to save her from being captured. The garden also features three other figures that seem to dance as they are transformed from women into trees. This particular garden was sponsored by the Union League Club of Chicago, which has done much to promote artists over its long history.

Cloud Gate

Anish Kapoor's *Cloud Gate* is just one of many outdoor works of art within Millennium Park, but it is undoubtedly the crowd favorite. It was unveiled in 2004 in the SBC Plaza, and in no time at all it became one of the most successful contemporary works of art in America. According to Kapoor, an artist born in India who lives in Great Britain, the piece was actually inspired by liquid mercury.

The 33-foot-tall, 66-foot-long sculpture is one of the largest in the world. Composed of 168 stainless steel plates, each weighing about 1,700 pounds, *Cloud Gate* weighs in at a mind-boggling 110 tons. The original plan was to construct the work off-site, but it was soon realized that it would be more time (not to mention energy) efficient to ship the parts to the plaza and assemble them there. This made for a fascinating spectacle for Chicagoans, except for the few months in late 2004 and early 2005, when it was taken off view temporarily. During that time, an enormous shelter was built over the sculpture while workers ground out the seams between the pieces. After that was finished, the whole surface could finally be polished to a mirror-like shine, as it is seen today.

Due to its elliptical-like arch, the ground level of the work reflects only the park—and the viewer, albeit in an eery, carnival mirror-like fashion. From a distance, one sees also the sculpture's upper level, which seems to bring the clouds, skyscrapers, and all manner of other out-of-reach things down to earth. Kapoor designed *Cloud Gate* for public interaction, though, and visitors are able not just to observe, but to *experience* the work by walking through and around it. Truly, *Cloud Gate* interacts with its surroundings and with the citizens in a way that is unprecedented in modern cities, and that could not be more in keeping with the civic spirit of Millenium Park itself. Chicagoans even took it upon themselves to name the piece before the artist: In the earliest stages of planning, a rendering of the yet-to-be-named work appeared in the newspaper. The nameless preview gave Chicagoans an opportunity to speculate themselves and, by the time Kapoor finally named the work *Cloud Gate*, citizens had already taken to calling it "the jellybean." Visitors who ask locals how to get to the sculpture Cloud Gate might be met with confused looks. Those who ask for "the jellybean," however, will be sent straight away to the new and beloved icon.

Wrigley Square

Since it opened, locals and visitors have been crowding into Millennium Park to check out all it has to offer, and most of them stumble on Wrigley Square sooner or later. Located at Michigan Avenue and Randolph Street, the square's open, tree-lined space is the cornerstone of the park, offering a place for people to congregate in attractive surroundings. Outdoor photography and art exhibits both local and international, as well as the occasional summer performance, draw those gatherers with great success, and have already earned Wrigley Square a reputation for "outdoor culture."

Few who gather there are actually conscious of the fact that they're perpetuating a long Chicago tradition. Decades ago, Edward Bennett first realized some of his design for Grant Park on this very corner. Under his supervision, the South Park District erected the original peristyle—a semi-circular collection of columns that encloses a court—and balustrades lining a promenade in 1917. Back then, too, people often met at this glorious, neoclassical landmark, and it was a much-loved feature of the park.

Unfortunately, the original peristyle was removed in 1953 during construction of an underground garage. However, Wrigley Square is now the site of the Millennium Monument, which drew on the earlier peristyle for inspiration. In addition to recalling the park's earlier history, it lists the private-sector donors who made contributions of more than $1 million for the development of Millennium Park. Private donors provided more than $100 million for the spectacular inner-city enhancements, making the park a model of public and private cooperation. This relationship is at the heart of Millennium Park and its larger civic function, and the Millenium Monument is the park's best symbol of that innovative spirit.

The Pritzker Pavilion

In the late 1990s, when the discussion of a Millennium Park began, people were intrigued by the city's plan to create parkland out of what had been railyards for almost 150 years. But when it was announced that Frank O. Gehry would design a new band shell for the city in the park, the excitement was nearly too much to contain. Gehry had caused an international sensation with his design for the Guggenheim Museum in Bilbao, Spain, which is extraordinary for its unusual curved, sculptural lines—now recognized as Gehry's signature design.

After years of anxious waiting, finally, in July 2004, the much-anticipated, Gehry-designed Music Pavilion was dedicated to the Pritzker family. Gehry's design is simply spectacular, with stainless-steel ribbons curling about and reaching into the sky almost forty feet above the pavilion. Especially when illuminated at night, the pavilion is an absolute triumph, reminding Chicagoans that any work of art by Gehry is worth the agonizing, suspenseful wait.

Although much of the anticipation surrounding Millenium Park focused on the Pritzker Pavilion, one of the park's real surprises is the trellis that extends from the pavilion to crisscross the lawn. It is the work of Skidmore, Owings and Merrill, Associates, the architectural firm responsible for the park's design and much of its engineering. The trellis is not only unusual and artistic, but also functional, as it provides support for the pavilion's state-of-the art lighting and sound system. The sound system uses digitally processed sound to create an excellent acoustic setting, and is the most sophisticated outdoor sound system of its type in the world. The trellis creates an altogether spectacular inte-

Though not technically part of Frank Gehry's pavilion, the trellis extending out from the pavilion supports its state-of-the-art lighting and sound systems and creates a sort of "shelter" for those enjoying the action on stage.

101

rior/exterior space, serving as a kind of "room" in the midst of Millennium Park, a "shelter" of sorts for the audiences, loafers, and picnickers that make use of the lawn.

With seating for 4,000 and 95,000 square feet of lawn (which can accommodate 11,000 more), the music pavilion has become the most natural place in the city to hold outdoor concerts and shows. The Grant Park Orchestra and Chorus, for instance, has already performed several times at the Pritzker Pavilion, including at the 2004 July 4th concert and fireworks display, which drew over a million people. The concert featured patriotic songs, including *The Star Spangled Banner* and John Phillip Sousa's *Stars and Stripes Forever*, as well as crowd favorites, like music from the popular movie *The Lord of the Rings*. That same year, a great honor was bestowed upon the Pritzker Pavilion when it was named the new home of the Grant Park Music Festival, one of the great musical institutions in America. James C. Petrillo, president of the Chicago Federation of Musicians from 1922 to 1962, worked to establish the annual festival in Grant Park. On July 1, 1935, his success was marked with the debut performance of Wagner's *Tannhauser* in an Art Deco band shell on the south end of Grant Park. The festival's first season consisted of 66 evening concerts, 26 symphonic programs, and 40 band concerts. The free concerts attracted tens of thousands of listeners, and the good cause drew the biggest stars of the day, including violinist Jascha Heifetz, conductor Andre Kostelanetz, and soprano Lily Pons. Today, the Grant Park Music Festival is the nation's only remaining free, municipally funded, outdoor classical music series—and it's only to be enjoyed at Pritzker.

The Crown Fountain

The Crown Fountain has emerged as one of the most unusual and surprising "enhancements" in Millenium Park—not to mention a crowd favorite. The Barcelona-native Jaume Plensa is a world-renowned sculptor who has lived and worked in a number of cities, including Berlin and Paris. The fountain takes its name from its donors, the Crown and Goodman families of Chicago, who put forward the multi-million-dollar gift that paid for the enormous work of art.

The fountain is located at the southwest corner of Millennium Park, at Michigan Avenue and Monroe Street. This is one of the few points within the park where traffic on Michigan Avenue and passersby on the sidewalk are brought into close proximity with activities inside the park. Towering over both are the two 50-foot-high, glass-block towers that flank a black granite pool 232 feet long by 48 feet wide. The towers feature LED screens that flash changing images of light effects, alternating water patterns, and faces.

Whose faces? Chicagoans, of course. Plensa filmed approximately 1,000 locals for the project, and their expressions are what make the fountain sometimes joyful, sometimes jolting, and always whimsical. Not only can visitors get up close to the faces, but every twelve minutes, just before the image on the towers changes, the face purses its lips and a jet of water shoots out from right between them. Then, the image dissolves and water cascades down from all sides of the towers. At the change of cycles, park-goers and passersby tend to gather in rapt attention, and in warm weather anxiously await the jet of cool water. Children step out onto the thick slab of water that unites the two towers, splashing as they make their way out to explore the area, and are always ready for the next arched spray.

Plensa's fountain has thoroughly transformed the idea of what a park fountain should be. Since the very first fountain in human history, fountains have always been static forms. With the Crown Fountain, Plensa proved that the

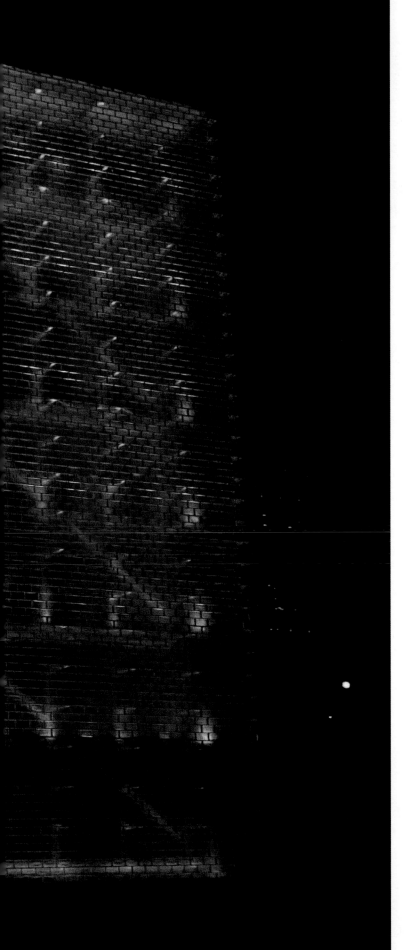

changing and moving images made possible by technology are good things in a fountain—at least according to the public. Much like Kapoor's *Cloud Gate* sculpture, Plensa has talked about the Crown Fountain as an environment in which people can interact with the work of art. Such interactive installments in Millenium Park may very well be a reflection of modern society, in which individuals feel increasingly isolated and lonely. At the same time, they encourage people to interact with the art—and in so doing, with one's fellow citizens—making them one potential solution to that problem. It is in this civic spirit that Millenium Park was built, and the embodiments of this spirit throughout the grounds are without a doubt its greatest achievement.

The Lurie Garden

The Lurie Garden is the namesake of Ann Lurie, a Chicago philanthropist who donated $10 million for the garden's creation and upkeep. The area was designed by an international team made up of Kathryn Gustafson, Piet Oudolf, and Robert Israel. Together, they created a distinctive area in the city by combining interesting plantings, unique architecture, and unusual lighting. The garden's location provides it with spectacular vistas of the city, including the Pritzker Pavilion, the Aon Building, and the Prudential Building.

In one sense, Lurie Garden is really a metaphor for the city of Chicago itself. A boardwalk divides the garden into two areas: one marshy and wet, representing the early history of the city, and the other a space to move through freely, like the city of today. The Ipe wood boardwalk hangs suspended over the water that runs from the garden's shallow pools, down a cascade of stones, and into grills, at which point it is recirculated. A step that runs the length of the boardwalk makes it a delightful place to sit and relax as well as to stroll.

Many find the boardwalk over the water the garden's most calming feature, inducing a sense of close connection to nature and the elements. The garden is a complex environment, though, and it encourages exploration and promises discovery. The space away from the boardwalk is divided among small, intimate areas that are reached by small footpaths, and grand, open areas that make much bolder statements. Each type of space serves its own useful purpose. For example, "the Extrusion Plaza," as designers call it, is an open area with large, Ipe wood seating platforms that provides plenty of space for larger groups to gather. Other spaces are almost hidden away, like sanctuaries from the crowds that form in other parts of the park.

A major element of the Lurie Garden's beauty is the great number of plantings that were carefully selected by the design team. In addition to the 15-foot-high hedges that create a partial enclosure for the garden, there are many unique botanical collections within, including one garden that features 240 varieties of perennial plants, and another full of flowering cherry trees. When one considers that most of these plantings will look decidedly different from season to season, the landscape becomes a very interesting work of art. What is truly distinctive about the Lurie Garden, though, is the foresight and faith in the future that these plantings reveal: The design team asserts that the park will not fulfill their vision until the plantings have been in place for about 15 years, meaning that this is a gift to Chicago that will only get better for future generations.

Chicago Learns: Cultural Contributions to the World

The University of Chicago: Former Walker Museum

Henry Ives Cobb is the architect responsible for the initial set of buildings on the University of Chicago campus, as well as for the campus' overall design. At the time of his commission, Cobb had designed the Fisheries Building for the World's Columbian Exposition and served as architect for the Newberry Library and the Chicago Historical Society. He was an influential architect in the city and a guiding force on campus during the University of Chicago's first decade.

Cobb designed a total of seventeen buildings for the university. In order to guarantee stylistic unity between all the buildings on the campus, he used the Gothic Revival style for all seventeen. Cobb was also responsible for organizing all of the buildings around a system of quadrangles, an arrangement that provides open space and common areas for people to congregate in away from street traffic.

The Walker Museum at 1115 E. 58th Street, completed in 1893, is one of Cobb's seventeen. It was named in honor of George C. Walker (1835-1905), who served on the university's Board of Trustees from 1890 until his death. Walker provided financial support for the construction of the building and encouraged others to make donations to build the university. The Walker Museum was originally intended to be a natural history museum, and so Cobb created a space that would have been suitable for the display of large skeletons. Ultimately, however, the natural history collection was given to the Field Museum of Natural History, and the university utilized the building for classrooms and laboratories. Today, after thorough renovation, the Walker Museum houses the university's computing services and School of Business.

Pages 110–111: Sunset over Chicago skyline.

The University of Chicago: The Chicago Theological Society

The Chicago Theological Society building at 5757 S. University Avenue was completed in 1926 by the architectural firm of Riddle and Riddle. Most of the campus' major structures were erected in the late nineteenth century, but through the foresight of the coordinating architect, Henry Ives Cobb, even buildings erected decades later blend in with the original structures. Cobb achieved this by using the Gothic style throughout the campus, and Riddle and Riddle's use of the same style makes the Chicago Theological Society building an excellent example of the technique's success.

The society fulfills the vision of William Rainey Harper, the university's first president and a Baptist clergyman. Harper believed that the university should be involved in the scholarly study of religion, because this training would prepare students not only for the ministry, but also for teaching and research. In that spirit, the Chicago Theological Seminary, a seminary of the United Church of Christ, prepares women and men to be religious leaders and to minister to individuals, churches, and society in general.

The society's building features the Thorndike Hilton Chapel, which is open around the clock. Nestled within the larger Gothic Revival building, the chapel's stained glass windows and cut stone are reminiscent of a small side altar in a cathedral. The seminary uses the chapel for small gatherings, individual prayer, and meditation. Adjacent to the chapel are the cloisters, a long corridor with one wall of glass doors that looks out on the stone-terraced garth—also a wonderful place for quiet reflection. In addition to the Chicago Theological Society, the University of Chicago has a number of other religious campus organizations, including the Buddhist Association, Hillel Center for Jewish Campus Life, and the Asian American Students for Christ.

The University of Chicago: Eckhart Hall

In 1930, architect Charles Z. Klauder completed Bernard Albert Eckhart Hall, located on one of the university's quadrangles at 1118 E. 58th Street. Klauder had gained fame for his work in the Gothic style at Princeton University, and he utilized that style for Eckhart Hall as well. In 1990, the university added a connecting bridge between the third floors of Ryerson and Eckhart Hall, which are also linked at the basement level. The bridge recalls the second-floor bridge that was originally part of the buildings.

When it was first built, Eckhart Hall housed the university's mathematics, astronomy, and physics departments, and signs of this early history are still readily apparent throughout the building. The arch of the building's doorway features bas-relief portraits of Sir Isaac Newton (1642-1727), who invented calculus, and Karl Friedrich Gauss (1777-1855), who proved the fundamental theorem of algebra. The building also features geometrical figures, as well as the twelve signs of the zodiac, representing astronomy. Perhaps more obscure are the shields with the coats-of-arms of three European universities: the University of Gottingen, Paris (the Sorbonne), and Cambridge. These three are honored due to the significant roles they played in the development of mathematics. Near the location of each of the original departments are also displayed the names of individual mathematicians, astronomers, and physicists who are considered notable in their disciplines.

Today, Eckhart Hall houses the mathematics department and library, which has a large collection of mathematical journals and texts. In addition to its undergraduate classes, the Mathematics Department offers graduate studies geared toward doctoral candidates. The majority of students in that program go on to teach at the most prestigious institutions of higher education in the United States.

Nuclear Energy

On The University of Chicago campus stands a massive, organic-looking work of art that people can't quite figure out. Titled *Nuclear Energy*, the piece marks the site of the world's first self-sustaining nuclear chain reaction—the achievement that ushered in the Atomic Age. The scientist responsible for the incredible breakthrough was the Italian-born Enrico Fermi, one of the leading researchers on the atom in the early twentieth century. His work in Italy had already won him a Nobel Prize in 1938, four years before the great advancement for which he is now honored by several Chicago institutions.

After attending the Nobel ceremonies in Stockholm, Sweden, Fermi took his family to the United States. Due to the developments in Italy after the outbreak of World War II, Fermi grew concerned for the safety of his Jewish wife, Laura, and so did not return with her and their two boys. Initially, he accepted a position at Columbia University in New York. In 1942, however, the United States government selected Fermi to lead the Manhattan Project at The University of

Chicago, where he was to work together with a number of other accomplished scientists in a secret government laboratory: a squash court underneath the university's football field.

There, beneath the grandstands of Stagg Field Stadium, the scientists built a nuclear reactor, called a pile, by arranging uranium, uranium oxide, and ultrapure graphite so as to maximize neutron propagation. And on December 2, 1942, at 2:20 Central Standard Time, the perfect conditions were reached for their goal: a 28-minute nuclear reaction occurred, which the scientists stopped by inserting neutron-absorbing cadmium control rods. Two years later, the Manhattan Project was moved to New Mexico, and Fermi went on to work on the creation of the first atomic bomb, which was detonated at Alamogordo Air Base on July 16, 1945. Less than one month later, an atomic bomb was dropped on Hiroshima, Japan.

After the war, Fermi returned to the University of Chicago, where he helped to found the university's Institute for Nuclear Studies in order to preserve the university's status as a leader in peaceful nuclear research. After his death in 1954, the university renamed the institute the Enrico Fermi Institute. The Chicago area in general has continued to be a region of intense atomic research: In 1967, the federal government located the National Accelerator Laboratory here. In 1974, it too was rededicated in honor of Enrico Fermi. Now called Fermilab, the laboratory is one of the world's largest particle accelerator labs and the site of cutting-edge experiments.

On the plaza that now stands where Enrico Fermi's squash-court laboratory was once located, the English-born Henry Moore's sculpture *Nuclear Energy* was dedicated in 1967 to commemorate the 25th anniversary of the scientific breakthrough. Some say that the 12-foot-high bronze sculpture looks like an atomic mushroom cloud, while others say it resembles the shape of a human skull. Whenever he talked about the piece, Moore never said what it depicts, but emphasized only the open spaces within the form.

Illinois Institute of Technology (IIT)

The Illinois Institute of Technology (IIT) has a long history of leadership in the fields of engineering and technology. The school's roots lie in a 1940 merger between the Armour Institute of Technology and the Lewis Institute (a technical school). The institute is best known for one of its early architects and educators, the still-famous Ludwig Mies van der Rohe, himself an international leader in modernist architecture.

In 1938, in protest of the policies of the Nazi government, Mies emigrated from Germany to Chicago and became director of the architecture department of the Armour Institute, continuing on at IIT after the merger. His buildings and teaching not only left his imprint on an entire generation of architects—he also left his mark on the IIT campus itself. Mies laid out the entire campus plan and designed many of the buildings in his trademark combination of steel, brick, and glass. Visitors to the campus often make their way to Crown Hall, now considered one of Mies' most important buildings.

Mies' 1953 Commons Building is incorporated into Rem Koolhaas' 2003 McCormick Tribune Campus Center, located at 3201 S. State Street. IIT built on its historic reputation for innovative architecture by selecting the Dutch-born Koolhaas to design the new center. Koolhaas' impressive design not only embraces Mies' previous work, but also the elevated train tracks above it. A central design element is the visually striking acoustic tube, which dampens the noise created by passing trains.

The Chicago Historical Society

The Chicago Historical Society (CHS) is one of the finest municipal museums in the United States. The organization dates back to 1856, making it one of the city's oldest cultural institutions. The society's first building was destroyed by the Great Chicago Fire of 1871, after which it was located for several decades at 632 N. Dearborn Street. Finally, in 1932, the society built itself a new home on the corner of Clark Street and North Avenue within Lincoln Park. The historic Georgian-style structure has undergone considerable expansion since then, most notably the large atrium entrance added in 1988.

When it was first opened to the public in 1932, the museum became a significant new attraction in the park, which already featured the Lincoln Park Zoo and Conservatory. The CHS' mission has always been to connect the city's past with the present, and it has always carried out that mission well. It has become one of the nation's leaders in historical interpretation, and it features impressive research collections on all topics relevant to Chicago history, as well as many innovative permanent and temporary exhibits. In the summertime, the CHS offers bus and walking tours to visitors and interested locals, and its gift shop and fine restaurant are popular places to stop by on a sunny afternoon. Those who can't make it to Chicago can still get a taste of what it has to offer by checking out its creative web exhibits online.

The Mexican Fine Arts Center Museum

The Mexican Fine Arts Center Museum, at 1852 West 19th Street, is one of Chicago's hidden cultural treasures. The museum is symbolic of the immigrant roots of the near west-side neighborhood where it is located, called Pilsen/Little Village. In the early twentieth century, the area housed immigrants from Bohemia, Germany, Poland, and Yugoslavia. Since the 1950s, Mexican and Puerto Rican immigrants have made their homes there. Much of the activity within the neighborhood centers around 18th Street between South Damen Avenue and South Halsted Street, an area with many restaurants and local shops.

The Mexican Fine Arts Center Museum is the largest Mexican art institution in the United States and one of Chicago's most innovative museums. Exhibits span a range of very different artists and include an excellent collection of art by the world-renowned painter Diego Rivera. Most popular at the museum is the "Day of the Dead" exhibit, which attracts a great crowd every year. The exhibit takes place around the Mexican holiday of the same name, and portrays the Catholic traditions of All Souls Day as well as Mexican customs that remember and honor the dead. The museum also has an excellent gift shop, which offers items related to both its temporary exhibits and its core collection.

The Adler Planetarium and Astronomy Museum

The Adler Planetarium and Astronomy Museum, located on the lakefront at 1300 S. Lake Shore Drive, was the United States' very first public planetarium. After its highly successful opening in 1930, it was decided to incorporate the building into the grounds of the Century of Progress Exposition of 1933 and 1934. Stylistically speaking, the twelve-sided domed structure is a drastic departure from its neoclassical neighbor, the Shedd Aquarium. The exterior features plaques by sculptor Alfonso Iannelli, who also sculpted the enormous Rock of Gibraltar at the city's Prudential Building.

Both the Adler and the Shedd underwent significant renovations in 1998, at which time the planetarium received a significant addition. It was a considerable challenge to harmonize the addition with the original structure, but most agree that the architects managed it nicely. The new area provides expansive exhibit areas and takes full advantage of its waterfront location by creating wonderful spaces from which to view the lake.

In an era in which scientists are conducting un-manned missions to Mars and to the moons of other planets, the planetarium is able to offer a great deal of information on the universe. The museum still utilizes the central dome from 1930 for projecting images of the sky, but the images become more accurate and interesting every day. Similarly, the museum's exhibits walk a fine line between new information and the timelessness of the stars themselves. For example, the exhibit called "Bringing the Heavens to the Earth" investigates how many different cultures used to look to astronomical phenomena for guidance in even the most practical matters of their lives. Visitors investi-gate how Polynesian navigators steered their boats using the stars, and how farmers in the Andes planted their potatoes based on the position of constellations. The planetarium also holds an important collection of astrological instruments that chronicle the world's study of the sky from ancient times to the present. Many of those tools are displayed and explored in the "Universe in Your Hands" exhibit, including ancient astrolabes, armillary spheres, and sundials.

The John G. Shedd Aquarium

The John G. Shedd Aquarium at 1200 S. Lake Shore Drive opened to the public in 1930. It was named to honor its major benefactor, John G. Shedd, a former president of Marshall Field and Company. The elegant neoclassical building fits in well with the nearby Field Museum of Natural History and Soldier Field. Today, the aquarium displays almost 8,000 saltwater and freshwater animals and is among the most popular destinations in the city.

As with most of the city's museums, the Shedd experienced significant growth in the 1990s, including the addition of its Oceanarium. The low-profile, sensitively designed addition provides the aquarium with some of its most spectacular exhibit space—not to mention remarkable vistas of Lake Michigan. In the main area that displays the Beluga whales and Pacific white-sided dolphins, it appears to visitors in the seating area that the salt-water pools extend out into the freshwater of the lake. It is an astounding optical illusion that is worth the price of admission all by itself.

Even with all the new stars at Shedd, the older exhibits still manage to attract their fair share of attention. Just beyond the main entrance is one of the oldest tanks in the aquarium, which displays the animals of the Caribbean Reef. Several times a day, visitors can watch a diver feeding and interacting with the fish as he provides information about them to the audience by microphone. Nearby are the tanks of animals from the Great Lakes region, one of the first attractions at Shedd and a particularly fun way to experience "native" Chicago.

Chicago Plays: Enjoying the Past, Present, and Future

Lincoln Park

When people visit Lincoln Park today, it is hard for them to believe that this was once on the northern edge of Chicago. About 4,000 people called Chicago their home at the time of the city's incorporation in 1837; by 1871 the city had grown astoundingly to a population of 325,000. For most of that period, Lincoln Park was nothing more than a municipal cemetery on the outskirts of town. In the 1860s, however, in light of the rapid outward growth of the city, city officials decided to close the municipal cemetery for health reasons.

The only marker within the park that remains from its earliest days as a cemetery is the 1858 Crouch Mausoleum near the Chicago Historical Society. It was designed by John Mills Van Osdel, who was arguably the most important architect in early Chicago. When the city made the decision to begin transferring remains to another location, the Crouch Family declined to remove the substantial mausoleum. In the past decade, excavation work has uncovered some remains a few blocks away that were also not relocated, albeit inadvertently. The city temporarily stopped the work and removed and re-interred the remains elsewhere.

The Crouch Mausoleum.

One of Lincoln Park's beloved swan boats.

Although the transfer of mortal remains would take a number of years, the city had already designated the area a public park at the time of the Civil War (1861-1865). With the assassination of President Abraham Lincoln in 1865, Chicagoans honored the fallen leader by rededicating the park in his name. Lincoln had chosen Illinois as his home state, and at the time of his election lived in Springfield, Illinois. Lincoln is honored in the park in one of the nation's finest sculptures of the fallen president, *The Standing Lincoln* (1887), by Augustus Saint-Gaudens, the best known sculptor in the United States at the time. In addition to Lincoln, many other fallen heroes are memorialized in the park. One of the most impressive monuments is that of Ulysses S. Grant, Civil War general and former president of the United States. Although his remains are located in New York City, patriotic individuals had sculptor Louis T. Rebisso and architect Francis M. Whitehouse construct the Ulysses S. Grant Memorial (completed in 1891) for Chicago's posterity.

Above: Lincoln Park Conservatory and its colorful gardens.

Left: Chilean flamingos at Lincoln Park Zoo.

In the same year that Augustus Saint-Gaudens sculpted *The Standing Lincoln*, he and his pupil Frederick William MacMonnies created Storks at Play, a fountain that was one of the early works of art to grace the park. Both works were commissioned with funds from the Chicago businessman Eli Bates, who left the city a bequest to erect a fountain and a statue of Abraham Lincoln in the park. Today the fountain is better known to locals as the Eli Bates Fountain, and is an extremely popular place to sit and read, pose for wedding photos, or to gather for a birthday party.

Eli Bates Fountain is situated between the Lincoln Park Conservatory and the western entrance to the Lincoln Park Zoo, two more very popular spots in Lincoln Park. The conservatory, located on Stockton Drive between Belden Avenue and Fullerton Parkway, dates back to 1894, and the glorious French garden leading up to it dates back to the late 1880s. The conservatory is a welcome break from the bustle of the city, especially in the winter, when it offers a breath of spring in what can often be a cold and wind-blown landscape. Within easy walking distance of the conservatory is North Pond Café, another great place to warm up or just relax a little. The building formerly served as a warming house for ice skaters, but has been converted into a fine dining restaurant within the last decade. It features superior exterior views and a fine Arts and Crafts style interior.

On the other side of the fountain is the Lincoln Park Zoo, one of the city's most visited sites—partially because of the free admission. The zoo had its start in 1868 when New York's Central Park donated two swans as a gift to the budding park. In the years to come, a succession of directors would oversee a good number of additions, including the famed Lion and Primate Houses. One of the zoo's most well-known directors was Marlin Perkins, who gained fame

Eli Bates Fountain in Lincoln Park.

for his role in Mutual of Omaha's *Wild Kingdom* and *Zoo Parade* programs. He also encouraged the development of the Children's Zoo and the now-famous Farm-in-the-Zoo.

Today, the Zoological Society manages the zoo for the Chicago Park District, which retains ownership of the site. The zoo now features a small mammal house, bird house, and penguin and seabird house, as well as many other habitats for animals. The Lincoln Park Zoo has seen many more modern additions since the Lion and Primate Houses, including the new Wild Things! gift shop and a variety of dining facilities.

What is interesting at the Lincoln Park Zoo—aside from the animals, of course—is the institution's skillful balance of past, present, and future. For example, the historic Lion House, designed in 1912, is a finely detailed structure that features terra cotta tiles reflecting the area's theme. On the other hand, the state-of-the-art display areas at the zoo just get better and better each year. The new Regenstein Ape House is one of the great new attractions that brings together the old and the new within the zoo. Opened to the public in 2004, architect Lohan Caprile Goettsch's structure provides excellent facilities for the animals, and visitors get to roam in and around the enclosures. The Regenstein Center for African Apes also features innovative exhibits that offer a variety of ways to learn about the apes, their ecosystem, and how the zoo is studying and protecting them. Among the most impressive exhibits are the sculptures of the apes and the interactive learning stations.

Lincoln Park has been the site of a great deal of landscape work over the years. In fact, the original site has been significantly altered, and much of what one sees now is the fruit of Chicago gardeners' hard labor. Artificial ponds, trees and shrubs, and delightful walkways that meander through the park are some of the additions. Especially beloved are the swan boats on the South Pond, a fanciful reminder of the founding of the Lincoln Park Zoological Society, which began with a gift of two swans from New York's Central Park in 1868. They are another good example of the park's efforts to balance history with modernity, to look forward without forgetting.

Lincoln Park has always been one of Chicago's great open spaces, offering needed relief from the overcrowded city. It offers excellent recreational opportunities along Lake Michigan and in the park itself, but all close to downtown. This perfect combination is what not only attracts millions of visitors each year, but also makes it one of the most desirable residential neighborhoods in the entire city. On any given sunny afternoon, hundreds of thousands gather there to play sports, stroll, swim, visit the many institutions—or just to find some peace and quiet. As a result, Lincoln Park is famous and most loved for being a democratic space, a lovely verdant setting in which anyone and everyone can stroll, visit, picnic, and play together.

Apes at Lincoln Park Zoo.

Navy Pier

Standing proudly at 600 E. Grant Avenue on Lake Michigan is one of Chicago's great tourist attractions. Over a million people visit Navy Pier each year, making it hard to believe that, not so long ago, the area was nothing but a shed-covered and underutilized expanse on the lakefront.

Navy Pier originally opened in 1916 as Municipal Pier, but was rededicated in 1927 to honor the sailors lost in World War I. The pier was proposed as part of the 1909 Plan for Chicago drafted by Daniel Burnham and Edward Bennett. Burnham and Bennett were architects and city planners who developed a comprehensive plan to bring Chicago—and especially its lakefront—to its full potential. In accordance with their special concern for the transportation situation of the rapidly expanding city, the pier became an important terminal for freight and passenger traffic in the years between 1918 and 1930. During World War II it served as a naval training facility, and thereafter as a branch campus for the University of Illinois at Chicago, from 1946 to 1965.

In the early 1970s, the pier fell into disuse, but in 1976 the spectacular Grand Ballroom at the eastern end of the pier was renovated, which created a little renaissance of activity there. Then, in 1989, the Metropolitan Pier and Exposition Authority undertook a major renovation to revive the area, and in 1995 it again underwent considerable reconstruction. Today it houses a food court, restaurants, shops, and a 230,000-square-foot Festival Hall convention facility that is joined to the historic Grand Ballroom. This makes it a prime spot for small conventions, receptions, and other special events. There are also a great number of permanent attractions on Navy Pier, including the particularly popular

Chicago Children's Museum and the Chicago Shakespeare Theater.

Visitors who make their way to the end of the pier just beyond the Grand Ballroom are rewarded for the trip. On most days, a hearty wind unfurls the American flags that surround the building, boats both imposing and quaint pass nearby, and spectacular vistas of the city stretch out before them. In the summer it is even possible to take a boat cruise that departs from the pier out onto Lake Michigan.

The shop windows and the smorgasbords—and even the crystal waters—don't really instill the true magic of Navy Pier, though. That's what the Ferris wheel is for. Few visitors realize how appropriate the Ferris wheel is at Chicago's Navy Pier, but the world's very first Ferris wheel was actually constructed as an attraction for the World's Columbian Exposition of 1893. George W. Ferris, from Pittsburgh, drew on his training in bridge building to create the engineering wonder and, of course, bequeathed to it his name. Well over one hundred years later, Chicago's Ferris wheel still has the power to awe both riders and onlookers—especially when it is lit up against the nighttime sky.

Clarence Buckingham Memorial Fountain

The Clarence Buckingham Memorial Fountain, or the Buckingham, as locals call it, is a major destination for Chicagoans and one of the sites they frequently bring their out-of-town visitors to. It is situated in the midst of the sizable Grant Park, one of the most interesting civic spaces in the city. Many of the park's structures were inspired by Chicago's beloved "White City," the popular name for the collection of monumental, white, neoclassical buildings used for exhibits at the World's Columbian Exposition of 1893. Most of the fair's original, temporary structures had been located in Jackson Park, and Chicagoans had long desired to recreate some of the fair's glory through permanent improvements to the area.

In the nineteenth century, the park occupied a long narrow strip of land, but a landfill project between 1896 and 1909 significantly expanded the site. The filling in of land continued for the construction of The Field Museum of Natural History to the south and even for Lake Shore Drive, now one of the city's grandest thoroughfares. Plans had originally placed the Field Museum at the center of the park, but Aaron Montgomery Ward, a property

owner, fought and won a contracted legal battle to prevent its location where the fountain now stands.

The fountain is named for Clarence Buckingham (1854-1913), a trustee and ardent supporter of the Art Institute of Chicago, which is also situated within the park. It was dedicated by his sister, Kate Sturges Buckingham (1854-1937), who paid for the construction and upkeep of the fountain. The architect primarily responsible for the design of Grant Park, Edward H. Bennett, served as the architect for the fountain as well. Marcel Francois Loyau was the sculptor and Jacques Lambert provided the spectacular engineering. At the fountain's 1927 dedication, John Phillip Sousa, the great military march composer, performed.

Each spring, the turning on of the fountain is a celebrated event in the city. The display shows off the fountain's hundreds of spotlights and 34 water jets that pump upwards of 14,100 gallons of water per minute, culminating with a 150-foot-high jet into the air. For the rest of the spring and summer, the fountain is never lonely at night, when its especially impressive lighting draws swarms of tourists and couples in love. On a warm summer evening, when there is a cool breeze blowing in from the lake, the edge of Buckingham Fountain may just be the most refreshing location in Chicago.

Wrigley Field

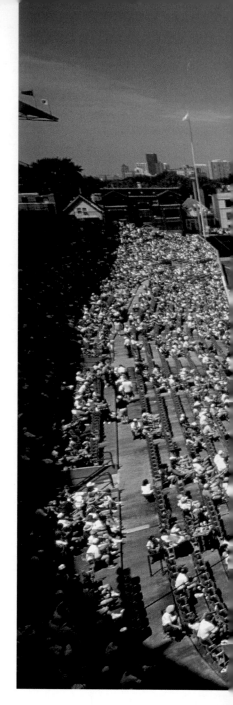

Located at 1060 W. Addison Street, "the Friendly Confines" of Wrigley Field comprise the oldest baseball stadium in the National League. Built in 1914 as the home field for the Chicago Cubs, the stadium is decidedly a throwback to an earlier era. Despite the appeal of the new baseball stadiums that feature retractable roofs, air-conditioned comfort, and state-of-the-art video screens, however, Wrigley Field still manages to attract over two million fans from all over the world every year.

Many of those fans are not even baseball lovers, but are drawn purely by the stadium's historic allure. The main scoreboard, for example, is an enormous, manually operated contraption, as opposed to a sleek, electronic device. Even the scheduling at Wrigley Field is rich with history: While most teams in the major league play their games by night, the majority of the Cubs' baseball games are played during the day, just as they were in the good 'ol days.

Most visitors are in fact sports lovers, though, and so any departure from tradition is usually a controversial subject. The stadium owners attempt now and then to blend a little bit of present into the past at Wrigley Field, and they're slowly learning where die-hard fans draw the line for them. For instance, when smaller, electronic scoreboards were introduced to Wrigley Field, they did not cause much of a stir, presumably because the manually

Statue of Harry Caray, one of the most colorful announcers in baseball history, outside of Wrigley Field on the corner of Addison and Sheffield.

Bird's-eye view of a summertime baseball game between the Chicago Cubs and the Colorado Rockies at Wrigley Field, 1997. © Joseph Sohm; ChromoSohm Inc./CORBIS.

operated main scoreboard was left untouched. On the other hand, when the owners began the installation of light standards in the 1980s, they met with great resistance. After the Cubs hosted and won their first night game on August 9, 1988, however, even their most conservative fans accepted artificially lit night games as a valid cause for rejoicing at Wrigley Field.

Cubs fans are notorious for their loyalty, and even those who don't have tickets frequently come to Wrigleyville (as the surrounding neighborhood is called) on game day just to share in the excitement. Some will be fortunate enough to make their way onto one of the rooftops from which fans view the game from outside the ballpark. A few with baseball gloves at the ready typically position themselves on Waveland or Sheffield Avenue in the hope of snagging baseballs knocked out of the ballpark. Some latecomers crowd around the ticket counters to battle for Standing-Room-Only tickets, entertained in the meantime by the Dixieland band that plays outside before games.

Soldier Field

Soldier Field, located at 425 E. McFetridge Drive, dates from the golden age of stadium building in America. The architectural firm of Holabird and Roche designed the original colonnade, which was constructed between 1922 and 1926. Like Navy Pier, the stadium was dedicated to honor the soldiers of World War I. It has hosted a number of significant events during its long history. Among them are the International Eucharistic Congress of 1926; the 1927 heavyweight championship boxing match between Jack Dempsey and Gene Tunney; and various football contests, including an Army vs. Navy football game in 1954 that attracted 100,000 fans. Since 1971, Soldier Field has also been the home of the National Football League Chicago Bears.

The Bears had one of their most memorable seasons in 1985/1986. That was the season that the team won the Super Bowl and became a team for the ages. The Bears had earned themselves such a good record that they had the home field advantage for the playoffs, and the playoff games at Soldier Field that year were among their finest. They managed to shut out the New York Giants and the Los Angeles Rams on their way to the championship.

The 1986 Super Bowl pitted the team against the New England Patriots. The players followed the lead of their hardboiled coach, the former Bears player Mike Ditka, and running back Walter Payton, who is one of the greatest players in the history of the game. Quarterback Jim McMahon, the

so-called "Punky QB" who showed up to early season practice with a Mohawk, was a highly touted first-round draft pick. William "The Refrigerator" Perry was defensive tackle. With a line-up like that, it was nearly impossible for the Bears to lose, and indeed, they emerged victorious with a final score of 46 to 19—the largest margin of victory in a Super Bowl up to that time. Although the team hasn't yet won another championship, that year they became blue-collar heroes for a blue-collar town, and they have remained so to their fans ever since.

As dear as their home field is to Bear-lovers, some Chicagoans have found the stadium on the lakefront a bit of a white elephant. When, in 2003, the city unveiled a new, ultramodern stadium situated within the historic, neoclassical colonnades, many Chicagoans grew even more unhappy with it. Some complained that it looked like a spaceship had landed inside of the old structure. Others, however, praised the degree to which the new stadium fit within the confines of the historic structure, as well as its wonderful new amenities and improved sightlines. The project also created a large under-ground parking garage, and the landscaping around the stadium was brought into harmony with the changes in the Museum Campus to the north.

The United Center

The United Center, located on the west side at 1800 W. Madison Street, is one of Chicago's newer stadiums. It replaced the much-loved Chicago Stadium as the home of the Chicago Bulls basketball team and the Chicago Black Hawks National Hockey League team. It was completed in 1994 by HOK Sports Facilities Group, the same organization that built the new Comiskey Park/US Cellular Field, home of the Chicago White Sox, as well as other remarkable baseball stadiums in Cleveland, Ohio, Arlington, Texas, and Baltimore, Maryland.

MICHAEL JORDAN

The United Center has quite a few luxury boxes, as well as a wide array of dining options. The stadium hosts over 200 major events each year, and in 1996 it even hosted the Democratic National Convention. Major sports games, such as the Men's NCAA Basketball Tournament and De Paul College Basketball are regularly held there, as is the Ringling Brothers and Barnum & Bailey Circus when it comes to town. Major musical acts, including Eric Clapton, U2, and the Rolling Stones, have graced the United Center stage as well.

One of the major attractions at The United Center is the statue of basketball great Michael Jordan near the building entrance. The larger-than-life sculpture of the sports hero scoring one of his famous slam dunks leaps from a 5-foot-high black granite base, on which are inscribed Jordan's player statistics. The piece is the work of husband-and-wife team Omri and Julie Rotblatt-Amrany, of Highland Park, Illinois. It was unveiled on national television on November 1, 1994, during an evening that included the retirement of Jordan's number, 23. Earlier that year, Jordan had announced his retirement after winning three National Basketball Association Championships. To everybody's delight, he actually returned to play with the Bulls, contributing to three more championship victories—in 1996, 1997, and 1998—earning the team six NBA championships in a single decade!

Jordan was born in Brooklyn, New York, on February 17, 1963. His parents moved to Wilmington, North Carolina when he was still a toddler, and Jordan grew up to play for Laney High School. He went on to accept a basketball scholarship from the University of North Carolina, then to join the Chicago Bulls. Contrary to what some might think, Jordan's career did not end with the Bulls. He became part-owner of the Washington Wizards basketball team, and even played for them. What people remember about Jordan is—and will always be—his spectacular career in Chicago, though, and as a result, people make their way at all hours of the day to see the Michael Jordan Statue in front of the stadium that he once called home. For his loyal fans, Jordan remains the greatest basketball player of all time.

Leon's Bar-B-Q

Chicago has become famous for its many trendy eateries, from no-nonsense bars and pubs to Chicago-style pizza and hot dog stands. Leon's Bar-B-Q is one more of those legendary Chicago locales. The owner, Leon Finney Sr., serves up high-quality meat that is cooked slowly over wood and drenched in his own spicy sauce. His restaurant is just one example of a larger trend of African-American eateries set up by Southern African-Americans who migrated north. Finney was born in Mississippi and moved to Chicago in 1940. He's seen his share of ups and downs in the business since then, but he can definitely be counted as one of the most successful migrants.

In Chicago, rib tips are the preferred cut of meat for Bar-B-Q and are often served with a rich, red hot sauce. Finney has three locations where his employees cut off the rib tips and marinate the meat. The slabs are then cooked in a smoker while the rib tips cook on rotisseries. As is well known (among locals, at least), each Bar-B-Q operation features its own sauces and seasonings that come to be associated with that particular family business. Finney creates his delicious sauce from Worcestershire, ketchup, mustard, vinegar, sugar, and other seasonings. Although off the beaten path, Leon still sells a staggering half-million pounds of rib tips a year—that's just how good they are at Leon's.

The Nine Dragon Wall in Chinatown is a reproduction of the one that stands in BeiHai Park in Beijing, China.

Chinatown

It's true what they say about Chicago being a city of neighborhoods, and one of its most distinctive neighborhoods is Chinatown. Chicago's Chinatown is the largest in the Midwest and one of the most visited of the city's many ethnic neighborhoods. It is easily accessible by the elevated train or by car. Most visitors come to eat at one of the many restaurants in the area. Patrons can eat at a restaurant that serves Chinese food as entrées, but many prefer eating dim sum, meaning that individual servings of food are selected tableside from steaming carts. For most visitors, a trip to Chinatown makes for a reasonably priced excursion to an exotic locale where English is not necessarily the first language spoken. For others, though, Chinatown offers a welcome taste of home.

The earliest recorded Chinese immigrant to the city of Chicago arrived in 1878. Soon, around 80 more men joined him and the Chinese population in the city began growing steadily. According to census records, 567 Chinese called Chicago their home in 1890, most of whom worked in the restaurant and laundry businesses.

Following right on the heels of the Communist takeover of mainland China in 1949 was the loosening of American immigration laws in the 1950s and 60s, both of which contributed to a dramatic increase in the number of Chinese in Chicago. Of the approximately 14,000 Chinese counted in the city around that time, a considerable few were living in the area around Cermak and Wentworth Avenues. That area, which had been an Italian and Croatian neighborhood before the Chinese influx, soon became Chicago's main Chinatown.

However, the neighborhood would soon not only lose housing, but space in general, as it saw itself hemmed in by construction of the Dan Ryan and Stevenson Expressways. To this day, the neighborhood has very little room to expand, despite the fact that the Chinese population continues to increase. Wentworth and Cermak is still the primary site of acculturation for new arrivals from Mainland China, Hong Kong, and Taiwan. Once the new arrivals gain better mastery of English and become familiar with life in the city, they tend to move out to the suburbs—but they are always replaced by the latest newcomers.

An arch demarks the neighborhood at Wentworth Avenue just south of Cermak Road. Many of the storefronts here are decorated with Chinese motifs, and locals on errands as well as former residents and curious visitors enjoy ambling along Wentworth Avenue and dropping into the interesting shops. Near the entrance arch is the On Leong Chinese Merchants' Association building, by far the most ornate structure in the area. It now serves as a cultural center. Toward the end of Wentworth Avenue is the Chinatown branch of the Chicago Public Library, with many books printed in Chinese. It is the library's busiest branch in the city. Because of overcrowding further south, the new Chinatown Square Mall was built on the north end of the neighborhood. It has its own distinctive flair with a mix of shops and dining establishments—definitely worth checking out.

The four Chinese characters suspended in this gateway are Li, Yi, Lien, *and* Chi, *which refer to the four basic virtues of a nation, as advocated by Chiang Kai-Shek, the late president of the Republic of China*

Billy Goat Tavern

The Billy Goat Tavern was "born" as the Lincoln Tavern in 1934 near the Chicago Stadium on the city's west side. The year before, President Franklin Delano Roosevelt had repealed the prohibition of alcohol and ushered in a new era of neighborhood taverns. The Billy Goat, however, was different from the rest. The bar originally attracted sports fans, but it built on its reputation as a place that serves no-nonsense drinks and straightforward food that fills guests up, and now it has one of the broadest, most diverse customer bases in the city.

Also contributing to the bar's reputation were the exploits of its original owner, a Greek immigrant named William "Billy Goat" Sianis. According to locals, the story of the bar's name goes like this: One day a truck was driving through Chicago's west side, when a goat fell off of it and wandered inside the tavern. Sianis—who had a great flair for promotion—adopted the goat, and even grew a goatee himself. His friends started calling him "Billy Goat," and so Sianis changed the name of the bar to the Billy Goat Tavern.

One of Sianis' exploits even supposedly explains the Chicago Cubs' streak of bad luck: In 1945, Sianis arrived at the baseball World Series accompanied by his goat. He had two tickets, but the ushers refused to allow the goat into the ballpark. Sianis refused to attend the game, and purportedly put a curse on the Chicago Cubs. Thus began the tradition of the Cubs' Curse, or the "Curse of the Billy Goat." Although many fans have tried to remove the curse many times and in various ways, the Cubs have still not returned to the World Series since 1945.

In 1964, the Billy Goat moved to its present location on the lower level of Michigan Avenue—a move that helped to shape its image. The bar is now tucked beneath the street, in the realm of delivery trucks and parking garages. The Chicago Tribune Tower is just steps away, and many of the newspaper's scribblers come to the Billy Goat to work in its corners or to spin stories at the bar. Mike Royko, a syndicated columnist for the *Chicago Tribune*, even brought fame to the tavern through his many references to the place in his columns.

In the 1970s, the bar became even more popular after the famous comedians Bill Murray, Dan Aykroyd, and John Belushi performed a sketch about the Billy Goat on the popular comedy program *Saturday Night Live*. In the sketch, the three made fun of the Greek accents of the owners and the fact that, no matter what patrons order, the order will always end up the same: "Cheezborger, Cheezborger, Cheezborger, no Pepsi… Coke." Today, a sign on the front of the tavern memorializes the skit with that famous line.

Given its reputation, the Billy Goat Tavern has become a must-see for many visitors to Chicago. It is now owned by Sam Sianis, the original owner's nephew. Objectively speaking, the food is pretty good, especially after a long day walking around the city. Those who come at odd hours often see a few of those hard-boiled journalists who still find haven in the corners and along the bar. As for that famous billy goat, he is respectfully remembered in the pictures on the walls of the restaurant.

The Berghoff Restaurant

The Berghoff Restaurant, located within Chicago's Loop at 17 W. Adams Street, provides a unique perspective on the past. It has become a sort of Chicago institution, a reminder of the important influence that German immigrants have had on the city's history and society.

The restaurant is housed in a building with an interesting cast-iron façade, constructed as a public hall just after the Great Fire of 1871. Inside, the walls are decorated with historical photos from the restaurant's and the city's history. The most interesting rooms are those that feature murals of the famous white structures—collectively known as the "White City"—that housed the exhibitions at the World's Columbian Exposition.

The Berghoff has been owned by the same family for over 100 years. Herman Joseph Berghoff came to the United States from Dortmund, Germany, in 1870, and began brewing Berghoff Beer in Fort Wayne, Indiana, 17 years later. At the 1893 World's Columbian Exposition, he sold his beer on the Midway in the hope that it would expand his market. Five years later, he opened a café just one door down from the Berghoff's present location. Like many establishments of the time, he sold his beer for a nickel and offered sandwiches for free. The business did well, even during Prohibition (1918-1933), when the café expanded into a full-service restaurant with "near beer" and soft drinks. Since Prohibition ended, however, the Berghoff's reputation for both great German food *and* beer has thankfully not been disrupted again.

White Palace Grill

The White Palace Grill is located on Chicago's south side at 1158 S. Canal Street at Roosevelt Road, between downtown and the ethnically diverse southwest side. Much of the surrounding area is still utilized by the railroads for railyards, but the neighborhood is undergoing rapid transformation. In this setting, the White Palace Grill is a link to the area's past. What's so unique about it? It's a small, family business in a blossoming flower bed of corporate chains—and it's been open 24 hours a day since 1939.

The diner may not look like much, but it is one of Chicago's unique dining experiences.

It is one of the authentic places that people expect to find in Chicago, a city known for its good, filling, down-to-earth food. It's the kind of diner that is regularly recreated in malls and shopping centers around the world, but White Palace is the real thing: an all-night, old-fashioned diner where people go in a city that never sleeps.

Owner George Liakopoulos recently renovated the restaurant, but he notes that some things just don't ever change: from the 1940s straight into the 21st century, people have been attracted at all hours of the day and night simply by good coffee and hot, "comfort food." Popular dishes include the grill's excellent eggs, great American cheeseburgers, and hot dogs. It's impossible to know who one will run into at the White Palace, but the regulars include third-shift workers and police officers, as well as college students from the University of Illinois at Chicago (UIC).

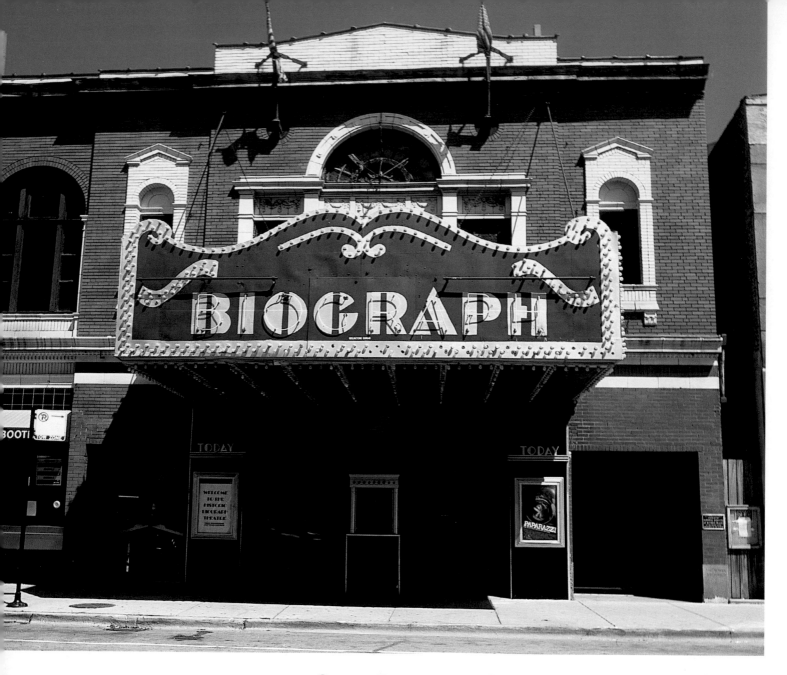

The Biograph Theater

The Biograph Theater at 2433 N. Lincoln Avenue has long provided cinematic entertainment for residents in Lincoln Park. Built in 1914, prior to the innovation of "talking films," the movie theater has seen a great deal of change in the city. It stands today as a reminder of the era in which a movie theater was still a wondrous thing, before the movie boom brought theaters to every small city and town in America.

During the 1920s, Chicago became notorious for organized crime, partially as a result of the federal government's 1919 ban on alcohol, known as Prohibition. Prohibition created an opportunity for organized crime to control the production and distribution of alcohol in the city, and it is from this golden era of the underground that popular culture has drawn its icons of Al Capone, the speakeasy, the Tommy gun, the St. Valentine's Day Massacre, and the G-men (government men).

Almost as an epilogue to the Prohibition era crimes, a year after Franklin Delano Roosevelt repealed Prohibition in 1933, John Dillinger was gunned down outside the Biograph Theater. Dillinger's bank robbing exploits had gained him infamy, but also a popular following among those who believed that banks acted unjustly by foreclosing on properties during the Great Depression. As one song of the day put it, "Some men rob you with a six-gun, others with a fountain pen." It is said that some who came upon the bloody scene dipped their handkerchiefs in the criminal's blood as ghoulish souvenirs.

Untitled Sculpture ("The Picasso")

Although its official name is *Untitled Sculpture*, this Chicago icon has come to be known as "the Picasso," after its sculptor, Pablo Picasso. Standing 50 feet high and weighing in at well over 100 tons, the sculpture is the centerpiece of Daley Center Plaza and, since it was placed there in 1967, has become a proud symbol for the city. Like the Richard J. Daley Center building behind it, the Picasso is made of Cor-Ten steel, a self-weathering steel that acquires a distinctive "rusted" patina with time.

The artist was decidedly mute on the inspiration for the work. Some have argued that it was based on his wife, and others say it resembles his dog. Picasso, who chose to stay in his beloved Paris even through the Nazi occupation, never traveled to Chicago or any other city in the United States. Nevertheless, he was intrigued by the idea of creating a work for Chicago, and ultimately offered the design and the model as a gift to the city's citizens.

In addition to serving as a favorite urban slide for kids, the Picasso is often the interesting backdrop for a great number of activities, including midday concerts and farmers' markets. The Loop has a number of modern sculptures, including works by Marc Chagall, Alexander Calder, and Joan Miró, but none of them is as beloved as the Picasso. To this day, however, it remains a controversial work as far as individual taste is concerned, and both locals and visitors tend to either love it or hate it.

Marina City

Located at 300 N. State Street, Marina City is one of the truly delightful pieces of architecture in Chicago. Betrand Goldberg and Associates created the innovative "corncob" towers and complex between 1959 and 1967. In an era in which so many Chicagoans felt turned off by the modernist architecture of Ludwig Mies van der Rohe, Marina City instantly became the leading rival of that architect's typical glass-and-steel office tower. At the same time, many people were moving out of the city, but Marina City proved that downtown living could compete even with the suburbs.

Marina City has become a model residence for young urban professionals, who want to both live and work downtown. Residents have access not only to the city, but to the Chicago River and Lake Michigan as well, and can even dock their boats just a stone's skip away from home. For drivers, the complex offers parking on the lower levels of the two sixty-story apartment towers.

Marina City is not just for residents, though. Those who work nearby— or just pass by—make frequent use of the buildings' bank, dry cleaners, and grocery store. With a restaurant, health center, theater, and office tower, too, the complex has become a bustling center of popular culture for Chicagoans in general. As a little extra perk for them, residents of the towers' condominiums bowl for half price at the 10-Pin Bowling Lounge, which features 24 state-of-the-art lanes. Still, the bowling alley's great video jukebox and lounge with extensive martinis and dining make a night out there a serious bargain even for non-residents.

Marina City's theater is now the site of Chicago's House of Blues, partially owned by comedian and "Blues Brother" Dan Aykroyd. In the 1970s, Dan Aykroyd and John Belushi portrayed Jake and Elwood Blues on the popular television program *Saturday Night Live*. The running skit became so popular that it was made into a movie in 1980. Aykroyd has gone on to be part-owner of a number of "House of Blues" clubs, including franchises in Los Angeles and New Orleans.

Before blues and drinks at the House of Blues, many dine on the famous prime ribs at Smith and Wollensky, Marina City's most popular restaurant. In good weather, the patio offers spectacular views, but even the dining room offers great views of the Chicago River. One of the restaurant's most unique features is its soundproof and air-conditioned kitchen that permits up to 12 diners to watch its saavy chefs and cooks at work.

In fact, Marina City hasn't even been just for Chicagoans. Americans from across the country occasionally recognize the corn cob towers that appeared in the *Bob Newhart Show's* opening shots from 1972 to 1978. The buildings were also featured in Steve McQueen's last film, *The Hunter* (1980), when a car flies off one of the building's parking structures during a car chase.

The historic building at 2120 S. Michigan Avenue in Chicago is more than the site of the old Chess Records Studio; it's also the home of Willie Dixon's Blues Heaven Foundation.

Willie Dixon's Blues Heaven

Originally built in 1911 as the McNaull Tire Company, the building at 2120 S. Michigan Avenue was significantly remodeled in 1957 to become the headquarters for Chess Records. Brothers Leonard and Phil Chess were Polish immigrants who recorded the unique sound of Chicago's African-American blues in the 1950s and 60s. By so doing, they had a significant influence on the musical history of the United States.

Chicago had a number of record companies in these years. VeeJay and Cobra were perhaps the best known, but it was Chess that changed the face of the music industry. The Chess brothers started their career in the nightclub scene on Chicago's south side in the 1940s. At that time,

the style of music they heard there embodied the emotional intensity of the "Mississippi Delta," a rough-and-tumble sound. Interested in capturing that, they went into the recording business, and in the end captured quite a few of the leading blues artists of the day. Under the Chess label they recorded Little Walter and Willie Dixon; a number of the early rock 'n' rollers, such as Bo Diddley and Chuck Berry, recorded under their subsidiary label, Checker Records. Several British rock groups also recorded in the building at 2120 S. Michigan, including the Yardbirds, who paid homage to their own musical heroes by recording in the same place they had recorded. Perhaps most significantly of all, the Rolling Stones recorded their *12 X 5* album in the building, a fact that still draws international crowds to point and stare at the building today.

Willie Dixon (1915–1992), of Vicksburg, Mississippi, played a significant role at Chess Records, both as studio manager and musician. Willie enjoyed some early success as a boxer, making his way even to the Chicago rings, but eventually settled on a career as a bass player. He worked for Chess Records from 1951 to 1956, then again from 1959 until the label's end in 1971. Dixon played bass with many of the most important rock 'n' roll musicians and blues players of his day, including Muddy Waters and Howlin' Wolf.

In 1984, Willie himself founded the organization Willie Dixon's Blues Heaven in the building that once housed Chess Records. His purpose was to "protect the blues artist of the past and to inspire future generations with the straightforward power of the blues tradition." In accordance with that mission, the foundation has donated thousands of instruments to schools, worked to create a number of educational music programs, and helped musicians regain royalty rights.

In addition, the foundation has worked with architects and crafts persons to restore the building to its 1957 appearance. Today, it is in excellent condition, a striking reminder of the powerful influence two young immigrants had on American pop culture. Many visitors to the city make a pilgrimage to Willie Dixon's Blues Heaven to honor the blues kings and early rock 'n' rollers who recorded at the Old Chess Studio—and it's worth the trip.

Outside the Willie Dixon's Blues Heaven building is Willie Dixon's Blues Garden, an open-air performance stage decorated with banners and silhouettes of famous blues performers.

Blue Chicago

Chicago earned its reputation as a blues town thanks to famous Chicago blues players like Muddy Waters, Little Walter, Buddy Guy, and Koko Taylor. The city used to be home to Chess Records, where many post-World War II blues musicians recorded, and it is still home to Dan Aykroyd's famous House of Blues and the Chicago Blues Festival, which honors artists not only from the city but from all over America.

The legacy of America's first blues artists is carried on today by a host of blues clubs in Chicago, most notably B.L.U.E.S., the Checkerboard Lounge, and Blue Chicago. Blue Chicago is one of the finest locations in the city for blues players to perform, and it welcomes both top local players and notable musicians who have adopted Chicago as their home, such as Eddy Clearwater and Willie Kent. Although Blue Chicago is, relatively speaking, a newcomer to

the blues scene, it has proved to be a favorite venue for locals and visitors. The club has two locations: the main one is located at 736 N. Clark, and the sister club is at 536 N. Clark. Thankfully, Blue Chicago has a very bar-hopping-friendly entrance policy: one cover charge gains admission to both clubs. Compact discs of the artists who play at the club can also be purchased in the on-site store.

Most of Chicago's blues clubs are really great places to capture part of the city's unique musical history. Some bars do cater to tourists, though, and here's how tourists can know they're not getting the authentic experience: if they play "Sweet Home Chicago" more than once an hour, it's a tourist trap. Those who aren't into running around looking for the real thing can always just stop in at Blue Chicago. They have only 100% down-home Chicago blues, all the time.

The Double Door

Chicago is a large enough city to have a number of those small, local bars that aspire to be much more than small and local. The Empty Bottle, the Elbow Room, and the Hot House are some of the more well-known examples, but the Double Door represents the best of the local music scene. The bar draws on the diversity of the city, honoring all the varied musical contributions of its past, yet always keeping up with the latest innovations. It's located at 1572 N. Milwaukee Avenue, near the unique intersection known as "six corners," where Damen, Milwaukee, and North Avenues all intersect. The bar takes its name from its two separate entrances, but most people use the main one on Damen, just below the elevated train tracks. This location in trendy Wicker Park might put some off, but rest assured: the Double Door attracts an audience as diverse as its tunes, and has managed to retain a laid-back, come-as-you-are atmosphere.

Although neither its exterior nor interior do much to recommend it, the Double Door has actually had great success getting the best local, regional, and national bands to perform on its stage. It's a place where locals come out to support their favorite bands and, in the past, that support has helped launch some of the Double Door's small-time gigs to national fame, including the Flaming Lips, Smashmouth, and Veruca Salt. Some locals still recount a memorable night in 1997 when the Rolling Stones made a surprise performance at the club. Perhaps solidifying its position as an icon in the city, the nightspot was featured in the closing scenes of the 2000 film *High Fidelity*, which featured actor John Cusack, a native of nearby ˙˙˙˙ Illinois.

Index